1

The Science of Getting Started:

How to Beat Procrastination, Summon Productivity, and Stop Self-Sabotage

By Patrick King
Social Interaction Specialist and
Conversation Coach
www.PatrickKingConsulting.com

Table of Contents

Introduction

I want to start this book with a story about procrastination, but maybe I'll tell you tomorrow...

When my mother was pregnant with me, my father promised to build a shelf in my nursery room to house all the keepsakes and memorabilia I would create as a growing human being: for instance, locks of hair from my first haircut, my baby teeth when they fell out, my first fingernail clippings, the bracelet that was put on me right after I was born, and my first pair of shoes.

It seems like everything parents keep of their young children is some form of refuse or garbage, but I suppose the sentimental value can't be discounted. The shelf was also supposed to have space across the top and bottom to act as a photo album, along with a ruler running down one side to track my height.

Sounds like a pretty good idea, right? Cute, even. At least that's what my father thought.

He conceived of this idea when I was barely the size of a peanut, which would place my mother somewhere between two and three months of pregnancy, roughly. The shelf ended up being built after I had already lost my first tooth, which would place me at roughly seven years old.

His grand shelf had a turnaround time of almost eight years, and it can probably be assumed that he wasn't off searching the world for the perfect tree to harvest wood from. It is also rather unlikely that he had changed his mind and wanted to wait for me to grow up so we could share the experience of building something together, though it's an excuse that sounds as good as any.

He just procrastinated and never quite got around to it. It always remained on his to-do list, but other tasks seemed to take precedence over it or have greater urgency. I later asked him how he allowed this to happen, and he said that it simply seemed like too big of a task and that everything else seemed easier to complete, so he would just perform those tasks first—washing the car, cleaning the gutters, cooking a pie. He might not have enjoyed any of those tasks, but at least they were relatively small and had a definite ending time, and he knew exactly where he could start.

Naturally, the next question I had was what motivated him to finally set his sights on finishing the shelf. It was completely related to his reason for not starting. Instead of viewing a shelf as an insurmountable task that would take up weeks of his time, he began to view it as something to do little by little. And he took this to the highest degree, buying some nails one weekend, taking some measurements another, and buying one to two pieces of the required lumber each month.

In other words, he took it slow and broke the overwhelming task into tiny steps that ultimately made it easy to say, "Oh, what the heck, I can do this right now." Despite my father's six years of delay tactics and absentmindedness, this is a story about how to slay the procrastination beast in a way we can all implement in our daily lives. One of the biggest weapons you have against procrastination is its natural enemy: making tasks almost impossible to skip over in the present moment. We'll cover that in more detail later.

Perhaps it is hereditary, but procrastination has also plagued me for years in both my personal and professional life. I'm embarrassed to say that I pulled multiple all-nighters in college and never seemed to learn my lesson. Breaking tasks into tiny steps was a big factor in defeating it, but understanding the psychology behind procrastination and why we can't seem to do what's best for us is what will get you to where you want to be.

Humans are many things, but acting in a way that is consistent with our intentions is not something we specialize in. It's time to dig deep into what happens in our brains when we suddenly want to clean the bathroom to avoid our homework. Getting off your butt to get started is not in itself a complex issue, but that undersells the calculations and negotiations we engage in as human beings.

Chapter 1. Why You're a Couch Potato

"Procrastination is opportunity's assassin."
- Victor Kiam

You have met procrastination before. It needs no introduction, especially when you've known it all your life. Since the moment you were old enough to recognize that you actually have the option to build a Lego castle rather than sit down to do your math homework, procrastination has been there in the background as the devil on your shoulder, encouraging you to do what is worst for you. It's like your shadow; you just can't shake it, it's always with you, and it's easy to forget about.

But unlike your shadow, it's dead set on ruining your life!

Now you're stuck with it and are having problems because it's starting to control you, like one of those relationships that started out fun and exciting but gradually morphed into something that just caused you unhappiness. *You know the ones I'm talking about.* So you want to break up with it to get your life back on track, but you don't know how.

The answer in finally regaining control from the demoralizing domination of procrastination starts with understanding what you are dealing with and how you continually get tricked into handing over the reins to it over and over again.

The term "procrastination" was derived from the Latin *pro*, meaning "forward, forth, or in favor of," and *crastinus*, meaning "of tomorrow." Its literal translation can thus be taken to be the moving forward of something to tomorrow or favoring tomorrow as the ideal time. Action is never for today; it's always another moment to be dealt with later.

For our purposes, procrastination is the act or habit of putting off something to a future time. It involves delaying what needs to be done until the last moment, often to the endpoint of not doing it at all. It involves a certain amount of self-sabotage and ignorance of any future consequences. It causes undue stress and anxiety, often at the pursuit of short-term gratification. It is responsible for an untold number of lost opportunities.

However, it's a mistake to assume that procrastination occurs simply because there is boredom or discomfort. They are parts of the problem, but in reality, much more goes into our lack of action. Just tackling an alleged lack of motivation and interest in something you need to do only shallowly addresses procrastination.

For instance, the thought of having to write out a 20,000-word research paper will certainly cause feelings of boredom and discomfort, so you may delay working on the task for as long as you can. A movie sounds more fun, stimulating, and comfortable.

The next thing you know, you've put off writing the paper until it's just a day before the deadline—which wasn't exactly a rational move, given the sheer size of work involved. You feel guilt and shame about letting things get that far, but you still didn't sit at your computer to start typing. You miss your deadline, lose your job, and your cat runs away from home.

Suppose the 20,000-word research paper was on a topic that you found stimulating and fun and comfortable. Are you so sure that you would wake up eagerly each morning, ready to start typing and editing? It might help, but it's still an unpleasant activity that you would rather substitute with fun. Also, consider how many things you currently avoid even though they are relatively fun and comfortable. They are too numerous to name. This means there is something deeper going on here that keeps you glued to your couch, physically or figuratively. In fact, there is a cycle that researchers have articulated, and this is the first of the reasons in this chapter that you are a couch potato.

The Procrastination Cycle

In some ways, the existence of a cycle is a relief because it means that beating procrastination isn't so much about reaching deep inside yourself and relying on your guts to get the job done (although sometimes that part cannot be avoided). It's actually about understanding the cycle of laziness and disrupting it before you get sucked into it.

It's the equivalent of understanding how to use a certain physics equation to solve a problem versus trying to solve the problem differently each time and sometimes just trying out 20 different possibilities. When you know what you're looking for, you're just going to be far more effective. In practical terms, this means that doing what you need to do will be much less of a struggle in the end.

There are five main phases of the cycle that explain why you tend to keep sitting on your butt even though you know you shouldn't be. It further explains how you justify sitting on your butt and even how you'll probably sit on your butt even more decisively the next time. We can follow along with an example of washing a car. You'll soon see how simplistic attributing procrastination to boredom or laziness is.

1. **Unhelpful assumptions or made-up rules**: "Life is short, so I should enjoy it and not spend my precious time washing that dusty car! Car washes are something you pay for anyway!"
2. **Increasing discomfort**: "I'd rather not wash the car. It's boring and uncomfortable. I know my spouse asked me to, but it can wait."
3. **Excuses for procrastination to decrease psychological discomfort**: "It's perfectly reasonable for me not to wash the car. It's so hot outside I would melt. My spouse didn't really mean it when they asked."
4. **Avoidance activities to decrease psychological discomfort**: "I will clean the bathroom instead. I'm still productive! I'll also arrange my desk. Lots of things getting done today. I did pretty well today, all things considered."
5. **Negative and positive consequences**: "Ah, I feel better about myself now. Cleanliness all around. Oh, wait. I still need to wash that car, and my spouse seems angrier this time…"

Which brings us full circle: the car isn't washed, and your assumptions remain the same if not reinforced, only this time there's even more discomfort that you want to avoid immediately. And so it goes on. Once you're in the cycle, it's hard to get over the increasing inertia keeping you from getting the task done.

Let's take a look at each of the phases individually. We'll start right from the top; this is where you are either failing to start a task or to complete a task already underway. You know you should do these things, and they are in your best interests. However, you've already made the decision against self-discipline, so what goes through your mind?

Unhelpful Assumptions or Made-Up Rules

If you feel like you don't want to start or follow through with something, it's not due to simple laziness or "I don't feel like it right now." It's about the beliefs and assumptions that underlie these feelings. What are some of these unhelpful assumptions or made-up rules?

My life should be about seeking pleasure, having fun, and enjoying myself. Anything that conflicts with that shouldn't be allowed. We all fall into this at one time or another. Pleasure-seeking is where you feel that life is too short to pass up something fun, interesting, or pleasant in favor of things that may seem boring or hard. Fun is the priority! At the very least, you believe that the current short-term pleasure is more important than a long-term payoff.

This is the true meaning of "I don't feel like it right now"—you are actually saying, "I want to do something more pleasurable than that right now."

I need X, Y, or Z to get to work, and if they are not present, I am excused. Sometimes you just can't muster up the energy to do something. You may feel tired, stressed, depressed, or unmotivated and use that as your "reason" for not getting things done. You have to be "ready." You need X, Y, and Z to start properly. You have to be *in the mood*. All of these so-called requirements were conjured by you; none of them actually reflect reality.

I probably won't do it right, so I just won't do it at all. You may fall into the assumption that you must do things perfectly every time or else it will be labeled a failure. This is a fear of failure and rejection, and it also involves a lack of self-confidence. You also don't want others to think less of you. And how do you ensure that neither of these things happen? You don't do it. You don't start it, and you don't finish it. There won't be failure or disappointment because you don't allow the opportunity for judgment.

If you feel that you need to do something that goes against your beliefs, you will only do it when absolutely necessary. This is a reality of human behavior, as is the fact that these beliefs are usually subconscious. So what happens if you are told to do household chores but you possess the first two beliefs of "fun comes first" and "I need perfect conditions"? You'll have fun first and then wait for a large set of preconditions, and the chores will go undone. The *rest* of the cycle is what *keeps* them undone.

Increasing Discomfort

When you are procrastinating, you're not totally unaware of what you need to do, and thus tension and discomfort will be created. Knowing you are being naughty does not promote good feelings.

You will have a range of emotions, all of which are uncomfortable: anger, boredom, frustration, exhaustion, resentment, anxiety, embarrassment, fear, or despair. The end result is that we are in an agitated state, and *we don't like feeling that way*. Something will need to change. Think of it this way: your brain doesn't want you to stay in a state of psychological discomfort— it's like standing on the bow of a sinking ship—so it deals with it the only way it knows how through the next two phases.

(Additionally, if the source of this discomfort is anything having to do with washing that darned car, that means you're going to avoid it like the black plague.)

Making Excuses

Excuses are the first way to make yourself feel better when you are ducking responsibility. You know you should do something, but you don't want to. Does this mean you're just lazy, tired, or entitled to no action? *Of course not.*

Admitting those would cause even more discomfort and tension than you already feel. So you construct excuses to remain the good guy or even victim in your situation— or at least not the bad guy. Now that's a comforting thought. What would you say to make your lack of action acceptable?

"I don't want to miss out on that party tonight. I'll do it tomorrow."
"I'm just too tired tonight. I'll start working on that goal later."
"I'll do a better job on that project when I'm in the mood to work on it."
"I don't have everything I need to finish the job, so I can't start now."
"I'll do it right after I finish this other task."

Now, if you uttered these to someone else, they might reply with a raised eyebrow and a "really...?" The problem is, these excuses are ones that you tell yourself. And you've probably used them so frequently in your life that the lines between your excuses and reality have blurred. You become unable to discern or tell the truth, and you unknowingly start to disempower yourself.

And while you're busy convincing yourself that these excuses are real and legitimate, you are smoothly transitioning into the next phase in the cycle: avoidance activities.

Avoidance Activities

Avoidance activities are the culmination of alleviating your discomfort and wanting to feel like you aren't simply being lazy. The internal dialogue goes something like this: "I'm sufficiently justified in not washing the car, but why do I still feel lousy about myself? I should *do* something..." Excuses on their own may not be enough, so you figure some action is still needed to lessen the discomfort and tension.

And so you act, though it's never what you should be doing in the first place. Typically, there are two types of avoidance activities. First, there are activities that simply distract you from the discomfort of choosing not to exercise your self-discipline or violate a belief or assumption. Out of sight, out of mind, and the discomfort is destroyed by going for ice cream or to a new superhero movie. This is distraction to the point of denial.

Second, there are activities that make you feel productive in some other way than the task at hand. For instance, if you work from home and are putting off a project, you will never have a cleaner bathroom than when real tasks are to be avoided. You might do an "easier" or lower-priority task. These avoidance activities allow you to say, "Well, at least I did something and wasn't totally unproductive with my time!" A fitting term for these activities is *productive procrastination*.

These activities do help you feel better about yourself in the short-term, but they don't move you any closer to where you should be and make the cycle harder to break.

Negative and Positive Consequences

Avoiding is an art. But when you avoid responsibilities, there are always consequences. Somewhere, something is slipping through the cracks. The negative consequences are more obvious. They can include increased discomfort, guilt, anxiety, and shame. You know you're not achieving (or taking steps to achieve) your goal, and this just makes you feel worse.

Another negative consequence is having increased demands on you. Your work may accumulate, leaving you to have to do the original task plus the additional compensatory work. And depending on the nature of the task, avoidance may lead to a consequence of punishment or loss. That punishment/loss may be in the form of repercussions at work, a missed opportunity, or failing to meet a goal. The chores go undone, and your lawn gets so out of control that you start to find small, vicious woodland animals in it.

Other negative consequences are related to this very cycle, where your unhelpful or incorrect assumptions or beliefs remain unchallenged, you become overly effective at making excuses for yourself, and your tolerance for psychological discomfort shrinks even more. These all perpetuate the cycle even worse.

Any positive consequences are illusory. You may actually feel better because you are sticking to your unhelpful assumptions. And you will probably get some enjoyment from your procrastination activities. They may be positive in that they feel good in the moment, but they are temporary at best. It's like shutting your eyes to avoid the bright headlights of a truck barreling toward you—you are just setting yourself up for failure in the long term. It's self-sabotage.

Both sets of consequences contribute to furthering the cycle. Negative consequences make you want to continue avoiding certain tasks, while positive consequences inject just enough short-term pleasure to disguise what's really happening. And they both lead you right back to the initial problem of sitting on your butt.

You can now see how this can become a vicious cycle. The more you subscribe to one or more of the unhelpful assumptions, the greater your discomfort. With increasing discomfort, you start to make excuses to avoid. The more you avoid, the more you *want* to avoid it due to both the negative and positive consequences. And you start back in with the unhelpful assumptions—probably strengthened for the worse at this point.

So what do these phases look like in a day-to-day life situation? Let's walk through the familiar chain reaction of events that you have unwittingly followed for years. What if you've always wanted to open an ice cream shop? Your friends and family know you love ice cream, and you're always talking about this dream of yours but you've never taken the plunge to start your own business. Maybe there's a cycle of procrastination contributing to your shop's absence.

What are the unhelpful assumptions you're telling yourself? A prime assumption would be about what might happen. If you quit your job and go full speed ahead with your ice cream business, you assume you'll be in poverty for the rest of your life. You assume being a business owner will be nonstop work. You assume you will lose a ton of money. You may even assume that you aren't smart enough to pull it off.

Thinking about these assumptions probably has you feeling pretty uncomfortable. You likely have some anxiety about such a big change. There may be some fear mixed in at the thought of quitting your job to go out on your own. You may be feeling overwhelmed by all of the things that go into starting your own business.

When you're feeling this uncomfortable, it's easy to come up with excuses for not moving forward. You can't open an ice cream shop because you just don't have the know-how. Maybe your excuse is that you don't know for sure if your shop will be a success. Or perhaps you feel like you don't have time to open a business.

So as a result of these excuses, you move into avoidance activities to make yourself feel better. Instead of going to the bank to find out about business loans, you watch the football game on TV instead. You get distracted. Or you get together with friends to talk about your idea instead of taking action on steps to move toward your dream. You feel productive in some non-movement way.

As for consequences of these avoidance tactics? One negative consequence may be that you miss out on an opportunity for a perfect location for your ice cream shop because you hadn't moved forward with your plan. One positive consequence could be that you enjoy spending time with your friends and you like talking about your idea, leading you to do this more frequently instead of starting up your business. Again, negative consequences create pessimism, while positive consequences create self-sabotage.

And here we are again at the start of the cycle as a couch potato. Obviously, awareness is a sizable part of the solution. If you can honestly admit to yourself that you are engaging in this cycle, you can gain self-awareness and put a stop to it.

With regard to the five steps of the cycle, you can't necessarily control the second (increasing discomfort) and fifth (consequences). The other steps (assumptions, excuses, and actions) are where we falter, and those you *can* control.

What are your assumptions based on?
- Are they legitimate?
- Are they realistic or far-fetched?
- Are they simply your anxieties and fears taking hold?
- Are you marginalizing the positives and amplifying the downsides?

What excuses do you tend to make?
- Are they based in reality?
- Are they honest and true?
- Is their sole purpose to keep you from action?
- If your excuse was true, would it excuse you from action anyway?

What actions do you tend to engage in?

- Do you *really* want to engage in them, or are they aimed at making you feel better about yourself?
- Is there something harder you should be doing instead?
- In an ideal world, what would you be doing right now?

Unfortunately, self-awareness is not a strong point for humans. But trying to acknowledge and buttress these entry points into the cycle of procrastination can help you succeed.

The Lizard Brain

Since the time of ancient civilizations, our ancestors have struggled with the dilemma of choosing to do what needs to be done over other, usually more pleasant, activities. We may imagine that our less industrious forebearers must have had days when they relaxed lying under a tree shade instead of picking up their spears to hunt or their baskets to forage for food. Hesiod, a Greek poet who lived around 800 B.C., cautioned not to "put your work off till tomorrow and the day after." Roman consul Cicero was also an early dissenter against procrastination, calling the act "hateful" in the conduct of affairs.

This is clearly a problem that is older than we give it credit for. Procrastination has been around since time immemorial. Has it been hardwired in our brains from the beginning?

Neurobiologists have found evidence that *yes*, the fundamental workings of our brains offer a recipe for procrastination. It's caused because it is *preferred*.

Remember that procrastination is the act of delaying an intended important task despite knowing that there will be negative consequences as a result of it. We have no problem recognizing that procrastinating is likely to be bad for us. Our human logic knows procrastinating is bad, but our human impulses are often stronger and so automatic that willpower or awareness alone can't save us from indulging them.

Procrastination is a failure of self-regulation. But why do we fail to regulate ourselves? Doesn't self-regulation improve our abilities to survive and hunt and work hard for a dollar? It does, but that's a modern conception; in the past, our survival came more from a dichotomy of seeking pleasure and avoiding pain (both of which procrastination handily delivers). We are ruled by these two factors more than we like to believe.

Imagine the brain as having two major portions—an inner portion and an outer portion. The inner portion is what some scientists call our "lizard brain," responsible for our most basic survival instincts. This region is fully developed from birth and controls our most primitive drives (e.g., hunger, thirst, and sex drive), as well as our mood and emotions (e.g., fear, anger, and pleasure). It's one of the most dominant portions of our brain, as its processes tend to be automatic, not to mention life-maintaining. This portion is called the limbic system. It quite literally keeps us alive because we don't have to consciously think about breathing or becoming hungry.

The outer portion, enclosing the limbic system and situated just behind our forehead, is called the prefrontal cortex. While the limbic system has been dubbed our "lizard brain," the prefrontal cortex has been identified by neurobiologists as the portion that separates us humans from lesser animals. The prefrontal cortex is in charge of our rational human functions, such as assimilating information, planning, making decisions, and other higher-order thinking skills.

So while the limbic system just lets us experience instincts and emotions automatically, the prefrontal cortex requires us to put in conscious and deliberate effort to be able to think, plan, decide, and ultimately complete a task. The prefrontal cortex works much, much slower, and we are generally conscious of these thoughts.

By now, you may recognize how these two major portions of the brain must be continually engaged in battle—a battle that you feel most intensely when you're faced with something you would rather not do but have to. In instances such as these, your limbic system is screaming, *"Don't do it! It doesn't feel good! WATCH TELEVISION!"* while your prefrontal cortex is trying to reason with you: *"Now, now, let's be reasonable; you have to do this."*

It's akin to what the well-known psychologist Sigmund Freud described as a constant battle between the instinctive, pleasure-driven id and the rational, reality-based ego. While the id cares only that you satisfy your impulses immediately, the ego has to consider the entire situation and the possible consequences of heeding the id's whims.

Thus, what experts are pointing to as the foundation of procrastination—the inability to manage drives and impulses—pertains to the inability of our prefrontal cortex to win over the whiny and spur-of-the-moment demands of our limbic system. The moment our prefrontal cortex lets up, we lose focus on a certain task and our limbic system is then quick to take the reins (remember, it's more automatic), moving us toward doing something more pleasurable instead.

Once we engage in that alternate activity, a chemical known as dopamine floods our brains. This is what creates the rush of pleasure we feel, and it's pretty addictive, too. We are drawn to activities that stimulate actual dopamine release, as well as to those activities we perceive will likely lead to that dopamine rush.

In other words, what leads us to procrastinate is not just the *actual* pleasure from those activities but, more importantly, the pleasure we *expect* to feel in choosing those activities over another. This is the scientific explanation behind procrastination—we anticipate we're going to feel better doing something else, so we go ahead and do it.

Our expectation of feeling good if we procrastinate is what drives us to put off our intended tasks for the moment and engage in a different activity instead. This anticipation of pleasure is the mental equivalent of drooling over a sumptuous dish; it whets our appetite for biting into the shiny yet poisoned fruit that is procrastination. Goodbye, homework; hello, old episodes of *I Love Lucy*.

If you are particularly work-shy, don't think that it's because you're a hopeless, lazy bum. Your limbic system might just be extra cunning, or your prefrontal cortex just needs a little more tweaking and practice in taking control of the situation (or both). See, your prefrontal cortex is like a muscle that can be trained and exercised to get better at beating procrastination. You can teach it to run strategies that'll boost your willpower to help you start and stay on task, jump past temptations, and hit the bull's-eye on your target goals.

A large portion of the lizard brain also pertains to impulsivity, which deserves a section of its own.

Driven by Impulse

Impulsivity means acting immediately on an impulse, whether it be a passing thought, a sudden emotion, or an instantaneous desire. Consider the common procrastination habits you may have. When you're bored with a task, it may occur to you how nice it would be to grab a bite first and relax watching an episode of your favorite sitcom, and the next second, you've abandoned your work and plopped down in front of the TV with a bag of chips.

Procrastination may have many other ways of manifesting other than that, but its many faces all have one thing in common: they arise out of an itch to do what feels good. Itches can be resisted, but not always and not forever.

If you recall, there's a constant battle between your limbic system's strong desire to seek pleasure and avoid pain and your prefrontal cortex's rational planning and decision-making controls. But while the prefrontal cortex's tasks require conscious effort to carry out, the limbic system's impulses are primitive and automatic. Unless your prefrontal cortex has been training for years and earned a black belt in limbic system control, it's likely to lose the fight against the more compelling and instinctive impulses of the limbic system.

Impulsivity is characterized by four broad characteristics, as detailed by behavioral researchers Martial Van der Linden and Mathieu d'Acremont in a 2005 study published in *The Journal of Nervous and Mental Disease.*

First, impulsivity involves **urgency**. You feel that you need to be in a rush to do something right this moment. For instance, you may feel compelled to check your social media accounts right now, and delaying it only fills you with mounting tension.

Second, there's **lack of premeditation**. You act without thinking or planning your actions, often with a relative disregard toward how such actions will affect you in the future. For example, even though you've just taken a break, you agree to a colleague's spontaneous invitation to another coffee break because you're finding your current task to be too monotonous. You fail to appreciate how unnecessarily taking yet another 15 minutes off-task is bound to affect the progress, timeliness, and quality of your work.

Third, there's **lack of perseverance**. You easily lose motivation and are prone to giving up on tasks that require prolonged effort. For instance, instead of staying at your desk long enough to finish the inventory report you're supposed to accomplish before lunch, you lose steam halfway through and spend the rest of the morning chatting with your workmates.

And fourth, impulsivity is characterized by **sensation-seeking**. You crave that feel-good sensation that comes from engaging in activities that you find thrilling, enjoyable, or exciting. For example, you can't sit still and endure the monotony of typing out data on a computer because you're itching to go online and experience the thrill of playing *World of Warcraft* again.

Now, add those four characteristics together—urgency, lack of premeditation, lack of perseverance, and sensation-seeking—and what you get is a person who's quickly derailed from working on their intended task and instead follows their spur-of-the-moment desires. The stronger these four tendencies are in you, the more likely you'll set aside what you need to do in order to go for what feels good at the moment.

It doesn't matter that you've planned to do a task for weeks. The only thing that matters to you, at that very instant, is that you get to do what you feel like doing. Your new impulse feels just as urgent to you as the intended task you've known about for weeks.

Impulsivity is a key feature of a number of mental disorders, such as attention-deficit/hyperactivity disorder (ADHD) and substance abuse. People with ADHD may engage in hasty actions or decisions without first thinking of their possible consequences. For example, they may agree to do a job without knowing enough information about it, use other people's things without asking permission, or intrude into conversations by cutting others off mid-sentence. They do these things not because they want to make a fool of themselves or intend to be rude, but because they lack the ability to stop themselves from acting on their immediate impulses.

If you believe you have the tendency to be impulsive, there are certain things you can do to curb that inclination. One strategy is to use the HALT method, a popular strategy originally taught in addiction recovery programs.

Before acting or making a decision, first be conscious of any feeling of hunger, anger, loneliness, or tiredness you may have. If you're feeling any of these, you're more likely to make rash, misguided decisions and act on your impulses that may lead you right into trouble. Thus, before jumping into anything, first consider the HALT factors and address any of them that may be weakening your resolve or influencing your decision-making.

Suppose you just came out of a meeting and you're angry at one of your colleagues because he threw you under the bus for a grave error on a project you both collaborated on. You go back to your desk and try to finish another report that's due within the hour, but you feel the urge to abandon it altogether. Before you do, recognize that your impulse to procrastinate might just be triggered by your anger.

Understanding this link, you can then consider how delaying the report will only further hurt your performance standing as an employee—which, given recent events, you cannot afford to let happen. So before jumping into any rash actions, recognize that the anger pushing you to procrastinate would not be the best thing to allow at this time. You may need to calm yourself first and change your perspective of the situation in order to regain control of yourself and not give in to procrastination.

Another strategy to help you be less impulsive is to recall the benefits of delaying gratification and perform a cost-benefit analysis for waiting. Before doing this, remember that you need to clear the HALT factors first so that your ability to consider the benefits of waiting won't be compromised. No one would want to wait any longer if they were hungry, angry, lonely or tired. Once you've established that you're free of HALT, consider how waiting at present would benefit you in the future.

For instance, imagine you're torn between completing a marketing plan summary at the office and bolting from work for three hours to catch a movie with your friends. While the prospect of relaxing in front of the big screen while sharing popcorn with your hilarious friends is definitely enticing, first recall the benefits of resisting that temptation and sticking with your task instead.

If you stay, you'll avoid getting into trouble at work, be able to cross off a major task from your to-do list, and get to fully enjoy the movie later instead of having to watch it while worried sick you might incur the wrath of your boss. Thus, delaying gratification appears to be the better option.

9 Procrastination Scales

We've gone through how the procrastination cycle and the lizard brain affect your work ethic, and now we can talk about some specific traits that need to be addressed and shored up.

Noting the connection between procrastination and the prefrontal cortex, researcher Laura Rabin of Brooklyn College delved into a closer examination of the relationship between procrastination and major processes in the prefrontal cortex.

Rabin's study assessed a sample of 212 students for procrastination, as well as the nine clinical subscales of prefrontal cortex executive functioning: (1) inhibition, (2) self-monitoring, (3) planning and organization, (4) activity shifting, (5) task initiation, (6) task monitoring, (7) emotional control, (8) working memory, and (9) general orderliness.

The researchers expected the first four of these subscales to be linked to procrastination. As it turned out, the results exceeded their expectations—all nine subscales were found to have significant associations with procrastination, as reported by Rabin and her colleagues in a 2011 issue of the *Journal of Clinical and Experimental Neuropsychology*.

Let's consider how each of these nine executive functions relates to procrastination. Perhaps you'll be able to identify yourself in some of them.

Inhibition. This pertains to your ability to be "in control" of yourself, to resist impulses, and to stop your own behavior when it's appropriate to do so. Inability to perform this function well leads to impulsivity, which typically manifests as acting without thinking. If you're prone to acting without first considering the consequences of your actions, then you might have problems with inhibition.

Lack of inhibition is a key factor in procrastination. If you can't control yourself enough to resist the impulse of going for an easier, more pleasurable activity, then you'll always just be choosing to do virtually anything else other than what you're supposed to be doing. You'll always be giving in to the temptation to engage in a more enjoyable activity rather than taking the pains of sticking to your to-do list.

Say you've intended to spend your first hour at the office researching ideas for your marketing proposal. However, as you sit down to work on it, your phone keeps beeping with notifications from the lively social media scene. Lacking inhibitory control, you fail to resist checking your phone and engaging with your friends on social media, and thus you end up procrastinating on your intended research task.

Self-monitoring. This refers to your ability to monitor your own behavior and its effect on you. Taken to the extreme, it's like being able to watch yourself from a bird's-eye view and understand why you are acting in certain ways.

Impaired self-monitoring thus inevitably results in a severe lack of self-awareness. It means you can't think about your own thinking, and thus you can be ruled by your lizard brain without even being aware of it. When lacking such self-awareness and the ability to think about your thinking, you'll be more likely to fall prey to destructive patterns of thought and bad habits, including procrastination.

When you're unaware of how you behave, you'll be less likely to even realize you're procrastinating. This is what happens when we pick up our phone to check an email and suddenly an hour of scrolling on social media passes.

Planning and organization. This comprises your ability to manage present and future task demands. The planning component of this function is about your ability to set goals and map out the right order of steps to get the job done. The organization component pertains to your ability to pick up on the main ideas of a given information load and to bring order to information. Together, planning and organization involve your ability to anticipate future situations and demands accurately and to take those into account as you lay out the steps necessary to achieve your goals.

If you lack the ability to set realistic goals and establish plans to meet those goals, you'll fail to understand the work and time needed.

As an example, imagine you need to work on completing a financial report due two weeks from now. Lacking effective planning skills, you don't break down the task into smaller portions and don't set specific hours you're going to work on it. You simply go through the days doing whatever's pushed under your nose (fonts, formatting, and type of paper to print on) and relaxing when nothing's due on that day. You put off doing the report until you realize, much to your panic, that it's due in two hours' time.

Activity shifting. This reflects your ability to easily move from one activity to another. If you're adept at activity shifting, you can make transitions effortlessly and tolerate change without getting distracted and off-track. This function also involves your ability to switch or alternate your attention as needed and to shift your focus from one aspect of a problem to another. Consider this your ability to be flexible in terms of both behavior and thinking.

A deficit in activity-shifting ability is linked with procrastination. After all, getting down to work basically constitutes a shift from non-working to working mode. If you're unable to switch from rest mode or from one productive mode to another, then you'll end up procrastinating because you just can't get yourself to switch to the other side. You'll stagnate at your original state, either doing nothing or continuing an activity you're not supposed to be doing at the time.

Say you've been diligent enough to draw up a schedule for the day. You've written that you're going to do some gardening from 8:00 a.m. to 9:00 a.m., then move inside the house and work on a manuscript from 9:00 a.m. to 11:00 a.m. However, you're fully enjoying and so engrossed in your gardening that you continue with it well past the time you've set for it to stop.

You end up spending your entire morning just gardening because you lacked the ability to shift your focus and energy onto the next task as scheduled. This form of procrastination can be tricky to spot and address, as it can look like you're making good use of your time when in fact you're not.

Task initiation. This pertains to your ability to simply start and get going on tasks or activities. It is what enables you to break the inertia of inactivity and take the first step on the task at hand—or on any task, for that matter. The first step is always the toughest to take. Task initiation also includes your capacity to generate ideas and problem-solving strategies by yourself. If this function is weak, you'll find it very difficult to begin anything. It will feel like you can see a long, winding road stretching out before you, but you just can't lift your foot to take the first step and walk along it.

You set a "start time" for each of your intended tasks, but once that moment arrives, you always find a reason to reschedule the start to another time. Or you just continue engaging in other activities you find more enjoyable.

It's 8:30 a.m. You say, *"I'll start at 9:00 a.m."* When you look back at the clock, you see it's 9:15 a.m. So you figure, *"Nah, I'll start at 10:00 a.m."* This carries on until oblivion.

Task monitoring. This refers to your ability to evaluate and keep track of your projects, as well as to identify and correct mistakes in your work. This also includes your ability to judge how easy or difficult a task will be for you and whether your problem-solving approaches are working or not. If your task monitoring function is impaired, you'll likely find it difficult to weed out which tasks need to be done first, or you may forget what you need to do altogether.

Deficient task monitoring is associated with procrastination. If you lack the ability to track your tasks, you'll fail to prioritize your activities properly, leading you to focus on the less important stuff. What's more, if you misjudge the difficulty of a certain task, you're more likely to put it off until later because you expect it to be easier than it actually is. A more realistic evaluation of the time and effort a task requires is essential to avoiding procrastination.

For instance, say you have a bunch of supply requests to review and approve. You estimate that it will take about an hour to finish all of them, and you've scheduled yourself to do the task during your last hour in the office. However, when that hour arrives, you don't feel motivated to proceed, so you put it off until tomorrow. After all, it will just take an hour.

Eventually, your attention is called as you've delayed the task for several days already and more work is piling up. When you finally sit down to work, you realize you've underestimated the time it takes to complete the task and regret all the time you wasted procrastinating.

Emotional control. This encompasses your ability to modulate or regulate your emotional responses. When your emotional control function is on point, you're able to react to events and situations appropriately. On the other hand, when your emotional control is problematic, you're likely to overreact to small problems, have sudden or frequent mood changes, get emotional easily, or have inappropriate outbursts.

Such inability to control your emotions is also likely to negatively impact your ability to control your thoughts. Emotions that run wild can derail the train of thought of even the most rational and intelligent people. So if you can't keep a lid on your emotions, you can't expect to be in full control of your thoughts—and your resulting actions—as well.

Remember the limbic system, that part of your brain that plays a significant role in your emotions, drives, and instincts? You're practically handing it the reins to direct your behavior if you lack the ability to control your emotional responses.

Imagine how a baby behaves. Because it's not yet adept at emotional control, it mostly just responds to the whims of the limbic system (e.g., when it's hungry, it cries without regard for appropriateness of time and place).

Let's say you're trying to work out solutions for a financial problem at the company. This undertaking is important but is causing you so much mental fatigue and distress that you decide to set it aside and pick up that entertaining phone of yours instead. The result? Procrastination.

Working memory. This comprises your capacity to hold information in your mind long enough to be able to complete a task. Your working memory is what enables you to follow complex instructions, manipulate information in your mind (e.g., do mental calculations), and carry out activities that have multiple steps. If you've ever walked into a room and forgotten what you went there for, you've experienced a lapse in your working memory. Scientists routinely estimate average working memory at having a capacity of *seven plus or minus two items.*

Poor working memory equals procrastination because you will literally forget what you are working on and why. It also lets you be more affected by temptations and distractions in your environment. You may have difficulty maintaining your attention on tasks that have multiple steps, leading you to stop halfway through and procrastinate instead.

Say you're tasked to review records of your project expenditures and prepare a progress report to inform upper management of your current project status. You had no problem getting yourself started on the task, but after looking over a couple of financial reports, you're finding it hard to keep track of the connections between all the papers you've been reading. Unable to remain focused, you shift your attention to the office chatter happening at the next cubicle. The next thing you know, you've joined your coworkers' conversation and have successfully abandoned your task for the day.

General orderliness. This refers to your ability to keep the things you need for projects well-organized and readily available, as well as to keep your workspaces orderly so that you're able to find whatever you need when you need it.

General orderliness brings about efficiency in the way you work, as it allows you to spend less time looking for things and more time actually working on the task.

If your work area or living space is not well-organized, you'll be more likely to find yourself in situations when you need to get up from working and look for things or even go out and buy materials you forgot you needed. You'll have veritable invitations for procrastination staring you in the face every moment of the day.

Distracted by these additional activities, you'll be more tempted to delay what you should be doing and instead engage in trivial activities. This applies even to the organization of files in your computer. If in your attempt to find one document, you need to sift through piles of folders with no discernable organizational scheme to them whatsoever, you're likely to come across other stuff that will distract you and lead you to procrastinate.

As a brief review, procrastination may arise from problems in each of the nine executive functions: (1) inhibition, (2) self-monitoring, (3) planning and organization, (4) activity shifting, (5) task initiation, (6) task monitoring, (7) emotional control, (8) working memory, and (9) general orderliness.

Some people may have a habit of procrastinating because they have trouble stopping themselves from engaging in certain activities (inhibition), others may procrastinate because they find it challenging to start (task initiation), and so on. Whatever the case, as with the previous section on the cycle of procrastination, it is imperative to understand what leads you to that point. Only then do solutions have a chance of being successful.

More often than not, procrastination can easily get out of hand and slowly eat away at your chances of achieving professional success and personal satisfaction. So how do you prevent procrastination from wreaking havoc in your life? Well, first things first: you've got to recognize the warning signs.

Takeaways:

- Procrastination has been around far longer than you or me. The term "procrastination" was derived from the Latin *pro*, meaning "forward, forth, or in favor of" and *crastinus*, meaning "of tomorrow." In everyday terms, it's when you put off something unpleasant, usually in pursuit of something more pleasurable or enjoyable. In this first chapter, we discuss the typical causes of procrastination.
- This begins with the cycle of procrastination, which has five stages: unhelpful/false assumptions, increasing discomfort, excuse-making, avoidance activities, and consequences. Focus on dispelling your false assumptions,

dissecting your excuses, and understanding your avoidance activities.

- The pleasure principle is important to understand in the context of procrastination. Our brains have a constant civil war brewing inside; the impulsive and largely subconscious lizard brain wants immediate pleasure at the expense of the slower prefrontal cortex, which makes rational decisions. The prefrontal cortex makes the unpopular decisions that procrastination is not a fan of, while the lizard brain makes decisions that lead to dopamine and adrenaline being produced. It may seem like a losing battle, but the key to battling procrastination is being able to regulate our impulses and drives—though not suppress them.

- You might simply be an impulsive person. Four traits make up impulsivity: urgency (I must do this right now), lack of premeditation (I don't know how this will affect me later), lack of perseverance (I'm tired of this; what else is there to do?), and sensation-seeking (oh, that feels better than what I am currently doing). The more elevated your levels, the more impulsive and procrastinating you will be.

- A helpful method for defeating procrastination is called HALT, and it stands for hunger, anger, loneliness, or tiredness. When you are facing a fork in the road in regards to persevering or procrastinating, ask yourself if any of the HALT factors are present. If any are, understand that you are already predisposed to making a poor decision and try to regulate your thoughts.

- It's been found that there are nine specific traits associated with procrastination: (1) inhibition, (2) self-monitoring, (3) planning and organization, (4) activity shifting, (5) task initiation, (6) task monitoring, (7) emotional control, (8) working memory, and (9) general orderliness. Generally, deficiencies in any of these nine traits will make an individual more susceptible to procrastination. To beat procrastination, we must perform one of the hardest tasks of all: thinking about one's own thinking.

Chapter 2. Your Procrastination Profile

"You may delay, but time will not."
—Benjamin Franklin

Before you attempt to rid your life of procrastination, you first need to be able to see *when* it's popping up in your life, *what* it looks like when it does, and *how* it is triggered. Not everyone procrastinates in the same way and for the same reasons, so knowing your personal tendencies and motivations is essential to later learning how to better handle yourself in the face of being tempted to procrastinate.

A doctor cannot effectively treat a patient without knowing what ails them, and similarly, we cannot handle our own brains without knowing what sets them into a frenzy of unproductivity.

Procrastination Typologies

Drawing mostly from research by psychology professor Dr. Joseph Ferrari, Alina Vrabie identifies five types of procrastinators: (1) thrill-seeker, (2) avoider, (3) indecisive, (4) perfectionist, and (5) busy. Try to get a sense of what characterizes each type and figure out which one personifies you best. You might be a mixture of multiple types of procrastinators.

Thrill-seeker. Also known as the crisis-makers, thrill-seekers live for the last-minute rush. As a deadline looms nearer, they feel more pumped up and ready to work. Instead of feeling frazzled under the pressure of racing against the clock, thrill-seekers actually enjoy the sensation of working close to a deadline. Their procrastination is thus more intentional than accidental, as they're likely to be aware of the boost in energy they feel as things get right down to the wire. If they're procrastinating, it's because they intend to. These are the people who claim to be able to work best under the stress of a deadline.

Obviously very confident in their capacity to produce quality output even with limited time, thrill-seekers feel that they work best under pressure and crave the adrenaline rush that comes with the experience. They deliberately leave the work untouched until the last minute so they can get that dose of adrenaline and thrill that they seek. This is part of what psychologist Mark Zuckerman calls "sensation-seeking," a trait more dominant in some people than in others.

For example, Lawrence is assigned to prepare a presentation that will introduce the company's new product in an upcoming launch. He has a month to work on it and make it an informative and engaging presentation. However, for weeks, he feels no motivation to start preparing the presentation. It was only a day before the scheduled launch that he felt a rush of creative ideas and energy to finally begin putting together the presentation. Lawrence is a classic thrill-seeker, procrastinating when there's plenty of time left and then feeling the rush to complete the task only moments before the deadline.

Avoider. Avoiders put off tasks until a later time in order to avoid being judged based on their output. While you may think that avoiders steer away from work because they find the tasks boring or tiring, in actuality, what avoiders are trying to run away from is the threat of failure or, in some instances, even that of success. They are typically self-conscious and highly concerned with what other people might think. Especially when given high-stakes tasks, avoiders shrivel up in fear of either messing up the entire thing or discovering what they're truly capable of.

Now, the avoiders' fear of failure is easy enough to understand—failure often causes people to lose confidence, credibility, and status. But fear of success? Why would avoiders be afraid of finding out their strengths and succeeding at their tasks?

The avoiders' fear of success is rooted in a sense of having to feel guilt and responsibility once they do discover the fullest extent of their capacities. If they work on a task and accomplish it with flying colors, they're likely to feel guilt for all the other times they performed below their potential.

In addition, they're also likely to feel a staggering responsibility to continue performing at their fullest capacities for the rest of the tasks they'll encounter in the future. This is an awful lot of uncomfortable feelings and thoughts to carry unconsciously, so their psyches attempt to save them from the discomfort by compelling them to procrastinate instead. That way, they're saved from the guilt and responsibility of recognizing their fullest potentials.

Say Nicole is an avoider who's tasked to come up with a charity project for her organization. She has a lot of ideas as to how to go about the project, but she acts on none of them for fear that they won't work out. Thus, instead of getting going on the task, she immerses herself in other activities, some of which are projects unrelated to what she's assigned to do while others are recreational activities— anything to avoid having to work on a task she fears she's going to fail at.

Indecisive. Indecisives procrastinate because they don't want to be held responsible for a negative outcome. Unlike avoiders, who fear either failure or success, indecisives mainly fear blame. While avoiders procrastinate to evade the judgment that comes *after* completing a task, indecisives procrastinate in order to shift the responsibility of doing the task at the *present* moment.

They attempt to put off having to make a decision or start on a task in the hopes that if they delay long enough, someone else will make the decision in their stead or the task might somehow be removed from their workload. If they weren't the ones who made the decision, then they couldn't be blamed if the decision turned out to be a mistake. If they never got to work on a task, then they couldn't be blamed for a negative outcome. Their fear of blame far exceeds their desire for recognition, so they prefer not to take the risk of deciding or working on a task at all.

Take, for instance, Mike, an indecisive procrastinator. He's been put in charge of an ad hoc committee tasked with developing a training program for company interns. His supervisor has asked him to submit a draft of the program three times now, but he still hasn't complied. He's delaying making the final call on important aspects of the program because he's afraid he might get blamed if it turns out to be a flop.

Perfectionist. Perfectionists delay tasks for fear that they're going to do things wrong. They've set standards for themselves and don't settle for a "job well done" or even "excellent job"; rather, they want nothing less than utter perfection. Now, you might wonder, if they want to achieve perfection, aren't they supposed to be the ones working super-hard in an attempt to perfect their work instead of lying about doing nothing or engaging in irrelevant activities?

Well, no. Perfectionists have set such high standards that the thought of attempting to measure up to those yardsticks fills them with paralyzing dread. As long as they don't touch a task, it still has the potential to be perfect. But once they start on the task, there's now a very real possibility of messing it up, with some errors potentially causing irreversible damage.

They're not necessarily as concerned with other people's opinions as avoiders are, nor do they have a fear of making decisions as indecisives do, but perfectionists tend to hold significantly higher standards than avoiders and indecisives do.

To escape the pressure of having to meet those sky-high standards, perfectionists simply leave tasks untouched and prefer instead to procrastinate. You would be right to also think that perfectionists are often people deathly afraid of judgment, just in disguise.

Say Sheena is tasked with updating the company manual with newly approved policies and procedures. Although completely capable of handling the job, she resists touching the manual for weeks for fear that she might deliver a less-than-perfect job. After all, the entire company is going to use the manual, so it needs to be flawless. Afraid of making mistakes, Sheena thus engages in other activities that will distract her from working on the manual, from reorganizing her office workspace to color-coding the file folders.

Busy. Busy procrastinators want to do it all, all at once. In their attempt to cover everything, they fail to actually get anything done. Their to-do list is crammed with tasks that all appear equally important to them. Thus, they typically start on one task, feel overwhelmed by the seeming urgency of another, jump to that other task, and then again think of another task they *really* have to get started on, jump on a different task again, and so on.

Busy procrastinators appear to be perpetually in motion but strangely never get to tick any single task off their to-do list. The main ability they lack is prioritizing, which leaves them fussing over too many tasks instead of working on them systematically. In reality, they're constantly in motion but not necessarily working toward anything major.

For example, Chris is an energetic manager who always has a long list of things to do, from following up with individual team members to writing reports and organizing capacity-building seminars. He always seems to be on the go, but somehow he is still often late for meetings and never submits paperwork on time. Chris personifies the busy procrastinator: always working but never done.

Typology Triggers

Each of the different types of procrastinators—thrill-seeker, avoider, indecisive, perfectionist, and busy—tends to have a different trigger for procrastinating. Some are greatly influenced by external activities and triggers in the environment, while others are more affected by internal mental and emotional factors.

Thrill-seekers are triggered by any activity around them that's irrelevant and enjoyable enough to allow them to push back their intended task to the last minute. Busy procrastinators are also triggered to put off tasks through external factors that allow them to start as many things as possible, but not finish any of them. Thrill-seekers and busy procrastinators are thus both largely influenced by action-based triggers—activities and prompts in their immediate environments that breed procrastination.

On the other hand, avoiders are prompted by the emotion of fear of either failure or success. Indecisives are triggered also by fear, but this time fear of blame.

Perfectionists are pressured by their own mental models of what they consider worthy work (i.e., only perfection).

Thus, what leads avoiders, indecisives, and perfectionists to procrastinate is mental/emotion-based triggers that drain them of the energy and motivation to work on their intended tasks. What's more, once they're considerably fatigued and stressed, their willpower to fight against procrastinating further declines, leading to a downward spiral of their chances of ever completing their tasks.

So as you see, there are two general kinds of triggers for procrastinating: action-based and mental/emotion-based.

Action-based triggers are environmental prompts and physical activities that support the continued practice of procrastination. For example, you may start clearing your desk to make space for the work you intend to do but end up wiping it down with disinfectant, organizing the papers you found lying about, and eventually cleaning and organizing the rest of your office. Remember that while sticking to a task requires conscious effort, procrastination is more automatic. Thus, when there are prompts all around you that trigger you to act on that automatic impulse, then you'll end up simply delaying what you need to do in order to indulge those triggers.

Action-based triggers involve what you find yourself doing when you start to procrastinate. For instance, you decide to go on social media for a quick breather from your task. What you planned to be a five-minute check on your notifications evolves into a two-hour-long break, scrolling on your feed and chatting with your friends. Another example is when you start your morning by drafting a schedule of what you intend to do for the day, then find yourself drawing up a schedule for tomorrow, the rest of the week, the entire month, and so on.

You might end up with your five-year career plan by the end of the day but discover you haven't even accomplished item number one on your to-do list.

Thus, it is important to be aware of these action-based triggers, catch yourself once you start to do them, and know how to deal with them appropriately to get yourself back on track. Try to look back on your habits and notice the patterns of procrastination you may fall into. Being aware of your go-to activities once you get bored or find the task too difficult is the key to catching yourself procrastinating next time.

For example, you may notice that once you lose interest or focus on a task, you automatically open up your browser and start entertaining yourself with YouTube videos. Knowing this tendency, you will later be more adept at catching yourself procrastinating and thus address it promptly or put in place strategies to make it harder for you to fall into its trap the next time.

The second kind of trigger for procrastinating involves your mental and emotional states. As mentioned, irrational thoughts (e.g., impossibly high expectations) and uncomfortable emotions (e.g., fear) may already be working to undermine your motivation to work. Add to that triggers such as physical fatigue, lack of sleep and exercise, unhealthy diet, and feelings of isolation from lack of social support, and you'll surely have lower resistance against procrastination.

For instance, say you're an avoider whose fear of failure is already taking up much of your mental energy to deal with. You're tasked to design a company logo for a client, but you delay working on it because you're unsure of your ability to deliver quality output. Over the week, you're also exhausted from your active avoidance of the task, as you took on numerous other less important ones that left you feeling mentally and physically drained.

Feeling like you're in no condition to get the creative juices flowing, you feel even more compelled to put off the task until a later time. Had you taken better care of yourself and saved your energy for your intended task, you would've been in a better condition to feel motivated to do it.

Despite It All...

While the numerous ways procrastination can cause problems in your life have been well-covered, you may ask whether there's any value to procrastination at all. Surely, nature can't be that bad at giving us a brain prone to procrastination when such a habit doesn't offer any value at all.

Moreover, the fact that procrastinating has persisted as a habit of humans from ancient civilizations to the present time indicates there must be an evolutionary advantage to keeping that practice going. If procrastination has been around for this long, there must be times when there's good reason to pursue pleasure rather than delay gratification, right?

Right! It turns out there are at least five ways procrastination can actually be useful in certain instances.

First, there are times when certain tasks and obligations simply disappear of their own accord, so you won't need to complete your intended tasks after all. This kept prehistoric man fresher and more energized. Evolutionary psychologist Dr. Doug Lisle explains that this was especially true in ancient times, when there was such uncertainty about the events that might transpire (e.g., people were more vulnerable to death by dismemberment and being eaten, etc.) that there was a good chance obligations and tasks would simply go away.

Consider a hunter expected to provide food for a family of ten. If a portion of that group suddenly died, procrastinating would have meant saving oneself from effort that would not have been necessary anyway.

In modern times, there's a lower likelihood that tasks and obligations will simply disappear. It still happens, but we often pay a consequence for procrastination these days.

Second, some types of procrastinating can push you to clear out the rest of your to-do list. This is because some tasks may seem so unpleasant to you that in order to avoid them, you would do anything, including the other tasks you need to do anyway.

On your list of tasks, you typically have things that you actually look forward to doing, things you're okay doing but not thrilled about, and things you really don't want to do. Given such gradation of the pleasantness or workability of tasks, you're bound to do whatever it takes to avoid that one task you find most abhorrent. It's a battle of lesser evils.

The next thing you know, you've cleared the rest of your to-do list, leaving only that one task for you to now focus on because you've got no other choice. Here, procrastinating actually helped your procrastination problem.

Third, procrastination can give you an opportunity to reevaluate tasks that may not be necessary or relevant. Putting off a task long enough can lead you to later look at it with fresh eyes and not even remember why it's on your to-do list. Recognizing it's unnecessary, you strike it off your list. Procrastination has freed you from investing time and effort in something totally needless.

For example, say you've written out all the activities involved in making a resource management plan. You listed every single task, failing to see that some of those tasks don't actually affect the end result. Fortunately, you've put off doing those tasks long enough to eventually realize that they were just backup measures to begin with.

Fourth, procrastination may be a function of your intuition, working to help you avoid jumping into something that might not be right for you. This applies especially when it comes to procrastinating on making decisions. In such cases, your procrastination is usually born out of uncertainty as to which would be the best choice to make. It arises out of the conflicting voices of your rational mind and your gut feeling, providing you more time to really figure out which one to listen to.

By delaying the act of choosing, you get to first think through the pros and cons of each option and disentangle your own confusion about the situation. When the moment arrives that you no longer have a choice but to make a decision, you'll be better prepared to make the right one because you've done your research.

For instance, suppose you're trying to decide whether to stay at your current job or take a job offer at another company. You delay the decision. In the meantime, you heavily research both options and consider the pros and cons of each. You discover that in a few months' time, you're up for a promotion in your current company, which would offer you better employment terms than if you took that other company's offer. So instead of jumping ship, you decide to stay.

In the above scenario, procrastinating on a decision turned out to be helpful to you, as it allowed you time to gather information and figure out the better option before committing to a decision. Had you made a choice right away, you likely would've jumped into something that wasn't the best option for you.

And fifth, procrastination may be your unconscious way of protecting yourself from the threat of failure. Fear of failure, according to Cal Newport, is what may underlie the compulsion to procrastinate. He explains that humans developed the ability for complex planning way before acquiring the capacity for verbal language.

So when you're about to get into a tricky situation in which you'll be prone to failing, it's unlikely there'll be a declaration in your head saying, *"This plan's not gonna work!"* Instead, you'll experience a lack of motivation to start, likely resulting from a biochemical cascade released by your body to restrain you from going the wrong way.

To decide where it will steer your actions, your brain calculates the likelihood of you succeeding versus the possibility of you failing at your endeavor. The greater the risk of failure, the more likely your brain will push you toward the road to procrastinating. It understands that failure will not only feel disappointing, but will also bring about loss of status among your peers.

To protect your ego and save your self-esteem from being crushed by such failure and loss of status, your brain compels you to procrastinate. By putting off a task that's likely to fail anyway, you curb the possibility of having to survive the blow of failure and get to buoy your self-esteem.

As an example, imagine you're planning to develop a mobile game app. You've come up with a few rudimentary ideas about what the game will be. However, there are already a lot of more popular game apps very similar to it, and your idea really doesn't offer anything new to the market. You procrastinate on developing the app, but while you think it's just due to plain laziness, in reality it's because your mind is aware the app will likely be a flop. Instead of having you labor on something that will only fail in the future, your mind deprives you of the feeling of motivation to even start.

In certain circumstances, procrastination does have its merits. It may save you from exerting unnecessary effort, push you to clear other stuff in your to-do list more quickly, prevent you from engaging in irrelevant tasks, and steer you away from making rash decisions that are misguided and likely to lead you to failure.

In conclusion, a number of warning signs can indicate a looming bout of procrastination. Depending on the type of procrastinator you are (thrill-seeker, avoider, indecisive, perfectionist, or busy), you may be triggered to procrastinate by certain actions, mental states, emotions, or even physical stress and fatigue. Impulsivity is also a key tendency that can derail you from focusing on what you should be doing and lead you to indulge in whatever feels good at the moment. To address these warning signs, you'll first need to have enough self-knowledge to be aware of when they're affecting you. Upon recognizing the signs, you can then utilize strategies that'll help you win against procrastination, starting with developing a better mindset.

Takeaways:

- This chapter is about the warning signs that procrastination is imminent. There are far too many to name, but there are a few common types that can be helpful to articulate and then diagnose in yourself. They come in the context that there are generally five different types of procrastinators: (1) thrill-seeker, (2) avoider, (3) indecisive, (4) perfectionist, and (5) busy. Each type has its own triggers, like the feeling of adrenaline and risk, avoiding rejection, and feeling overwhelmed. They can generally be grouped into two general kinds of procrastination triggers: action-based and mental/emotion-based. These speak to the physical environment and to lack of confidence and security, respectively.

- Finally, procrastination has been shown to be useful from time to time, even though it can lead to our downfall. It can improve your efficiency, clear out the rest of our to-do list, and protect yourself from hasty decisions and failure.

Chapter 3: Action Mindsets

"If and When were planted, and Nothing grew."
—Proverb

At this point, you've learned why you are engaging in self-sabotage. You should be able to generally identify a few reasons that you are a couch potato. It might be due to your prefrontal cortex being hijacked by your lizard brain, or it might be due to being unknowingly immersed in the procrastination cycle. You may have even identified one or two typologies in yourself.

But whatever the case, the time begins for real solutions.

This chapter entails building anti-procrastination mindsets—outlooks and approaches that get you off your butt to deal with the options you come across in more productive ways.

There are at least three ways you can build a mindset that's iron-clad against the ever-constant lure of procrastination: (1) mastering the physics of productivity, (2) eliminating the paradox of choice, and (3) finding the right motivation to kick-start action.

The Physics of Productivity

Who would have thought that productivity and procrastination could be viewed through the lens of physics, math, and equations? Bestselling author Stephen Guise found a way to do so using Newton's three laws of motion as an analogy to formulate the Three Laws of Productivity.

By dissecting procrastination as physics concepts and equations with identifiable elements and interactions, you'll get to identify the specific things you need to do or to avoid in order to add to your productivity and subtract from your procrastination. If you know the variables at work when you procrastinate, then you'll literally be able to single out a particular variable and manipulate it, as you're able to do in a mathematical equation.

The three laws of motion were formulated by physicist Sir Isaac Newton in 1687 to explain how physical objects and systems move and are affected by the forces around them. He's the guy who claims to have conceived of gravity after getting hit by a falling apple. These laws lay the foundation for understanding how things from the smallest machine parts to the largest spacecraft and planets move. And now applied to the science of human cognition and behavior, these laws can also illuminate the mechanisms behind procrastination— and how to manipulate those mechanisms to drive productivity instead.

First law of motion. According to Newton's first law of motion, an object at rest tends to remain at rest and an object in motion continues to be in motion unless an outside force acts upon it.

How this law applies to procrastination is glaringly evident: an object at rest tends to remain at rest, which means a person in a state of rest tends to remain at rest—unless some sort of force moves him or her into action. So if you're currently in a state of inaction with regard to your intended task, you'll tend to remain inactive unless you're stimulated into motion. Your tendency to leave that task untouched is thus a fundamental law of the universe.

But before you start to think being a perpetual procrastinator is a hopeless case, remember that Newton's first law of motion works the other way, too: an object in motion continues to be in motion, which means a person in a state of action tends to continue moving as well. So if you're currently working on a task, this law of motion states that you'll tend to keep working on that task.

So what does this mean in the context of productivity and procrastination? The most critical element of beating procrastination is to find a way to start. Find a way to get moving. Once you get the ball rolling, it gets infinitely easier to keep going until the task is done.

Now, the next question becomes, how do you get started on a task? Writer James Clear suggests following what's known as the two-minute rule as applied to productivity. The rule states that you need to start your task in less than two minutes from the time you start thinking about it. Think of it as a personal contract you strike with yourself. No matter what, you need to start within the next two minutes.

For example, suppose you're tasked to write a report detailing your department's project updates. To beat the inertia of lazing around the entire morning, commit to just jotting down the project title and objectives or expected output within the next two minutes. You don't need to think about doing the rest of it just yet. You only need to start within the next two minutes. This action will help break the inactivity that's been strapping you down, and once you've started writing things down about your project, you'll find it easier to keep going.

Another benefit of abiding by this rule is that you'll also be forced to break the task down into smaller and smaller steps, as giving yourself a two-minute limit for starting requires you to think in terms of more manageable chunks of work you can start quick and easy.

Note that the two-minute rule doesn't require you to pledge that you finish your task or even proceed with your task in an orderly manner. It doesn't need you to mind the quality of your output just yet; you can reserve the critiquing and refining of it for later. It just needs you to start, to get into motion.

This relieves a lot of the pressure that typically paralyzes you from touching a task and thus leads you down a path of procrastination. With Newton's first law of motion, you'll find that once you start, you will tend to keep going on your task. So rather than wait for an enormous amount of motivation before starting, just go ahead and start small. You'll find that your motivation will snowball into ever-larger amounts after you've started.

Second law of motion. Newton's second law of motion explains how a particular force affects the rate at which an object is moving. It is represented by the equation $F=ma$, which states that the sum of forces (F) acting on an object is the product of that object's mass (m, which refers to how much matter there is in an object) and its acceleration (a, which is the rate of change in how fast an object is going).

In other words, the second law of motion dictates how much force is needed in order to accelerate an object of a particular mass in a certain direction. And as illustrated by the equation, the relationship between these three variables—force, mass, and acceleration—is proportional. The greater the mass of an object, the greater the force required to accelerate it. Likewise, the faster you need an object to move over time (i.e., accelerate), the greater the force you'll need to apply.

So if you want to accelerate an object—say, a ball—then the amount of force you exert on that ball, as well as the direction of that force you apply on the ball, will both make a difference. If more force is applied for the ball to go left than for it to go right, then you can bet that ball will go left.

Still with me?

Applied to productivity, this means that you'll need to pay attention not only to the amount of work you're doing (magnitude), but also to where you're applying that work (direction). If you work a lot but don't focus all that work in a single direction, then you'll tend to accomplish less than when you direct the same amount of work to only one direction.

The amount of work you're able to do as a person has its limits, so if you want to get the most out of your effort, you need to start being conscious of where that work goes. As Newton's $F=ma$ equation teaches, where you direct your effort is just as important as how much effort you exert. Temptations, distractions, and lack of task prioritization all serve to scatter your energy and effort in different directions, so avoiding them is key to optimizing your productivity. Keep your energy focused.

Say you have a myriad of things to accomplish before the day is up—reply to five client emails, read and critique a lengthy research plan, and write a recommendation letter for a former employee.

Applying Newton's second law, you need to recognize that how fast you'll be able to accomplish a particular task depends largely on your ability to focus the effort you exert on that task and that task only. If you insist on scattering the "force" you exert by frequently switching tabs from email to research to letter-writing all throughout the morning, you'll be less likely to accomplish any one of them before the lunch hour. You may even just be switching back and forth on those tasks as a way to procrastinate on all of them.

To remedy this, apply the principle of Newton's second law: exert your force in a single direction for its maximum acceleration.

Third law of motion. This law of motion states that "For every action, there is an equal and opposite reaction." This means that when Object A applies a force on Object B, Object B simultaneously applies a force of the same amount, but of opposite direction, on Object A. For example, when you swim, you apply force on the water as you push it backward. Simultaneously, the water applies a force on you that's equal in magnitude yet opposite in direction, thus pushing you forward.

Applied to the science of productivity and procrastination, this law reflects how in your own life there are often productive and unproductive forces at work as well.

There is a constant battle, and everyone's level of balance is different. For those who are unproductive, their unproductive forces tend to win more often than not.

Productive forces include positivity, atmosphere, environment, social network, focus, and motivation, while unproductive forces include stress, temptation and distraction, unrealistic work goals, and unhealthy lifestyles (e.g., poor diet or lack of sleep). The interaction and balance between these opposite forces is what creates your typical levels of productivity, as well as your usual patterns of procrastination.

This balance could shift either way—it could lead you to be massively productive or to severely procrastinate. For example, it may take you just an hour to finish writing a report when you're feeling well-rested and confident in your abilities, but you may need a week to complete the same task when you're feeling stressed out and insecure.

Basing on the applications of Newton's third law of motion, there are two ways you can go about upping your productivity level and avoid procrastination. The first is to add more productive forces. This is what James Clear refers to as the "power through it" option, in which you simply find a way to pump yourself up with more energy in an attempt to overpower the unproductive forces inhibiting you from working. This strategy may involve such actions as chugging cup after cup of coffee and digesting motivational words through books or inspirational videos.

The "power through it" option could work well, but only for a brief time. The problem with this strategy is that you're only trying to cover up the unproductive forces that are still working to undermine your productivity, and this tiring task could easily lead to burnout.

As an alternative, Clear suggests dealing with unproductive forces directly through the second option, which is to subtract, if not totally eliminate, unproductive forces. This strategy involves such actions as reducing the number of tasks you commit to, learning how to say no, and changing your environment in order to simplify your life.

Compared to the first option, which requires you to add more productive forces, this second option simply needs you to release the reservoir of energy and productivity already within you by removing the barriers that obstruct it. As you can imagine, this second option is an easier way to defeat procrastination than having to produce productivity by attempting to add more productive forces.

For example, say you need to accomplish a year-end evaluation report for your organization's project sponsor. You're aware that you're the type of worker who needs quiet in order to think and work effectively, but your office cubicle is between two chatty colleagues. Instead of simply opting to "power through" the task despite the noisy and distracting environment you're in (i.e., attempting to increase your productive forces), consider relocating to a quieter area or politely asking your colleagues to refrain from disturbing you for the next hour or two (i.e., eliminating unproductive forces).

That way, you'll be more motivated to start and keep working on a task, not necessarily because you've upped your willpower, but because you've simply let the natural energy already within you flow unhindered.

Eliminate the Paradox of Choice

While most people tend to think that having choices is good—and the more choices there are, the better—current research on human behavior actually suggests otherwise. In a phenomenon that psychologist Barry Schwartz calls the paradox of choice, people tend to be worse off when they have more options to choose from as opposed to when they have a single course of action available to them.

For example, suppose your company offers multiple types of research grants you can apply for. Pressured to make the "best" choice among all your options and overwhelmed by the details and comparisons you need to sift through to be able to do so, you put the whole research thing on the back burner and leave it untouched for years. With zero additional research studies under your belt, you suffer career stagnation simply because in the face of multiple options, you've been too paralyzed to do anything.

Learning to deal with the paradox of choice is thus a necessary technique to beat procrastination. If you've established a mindset that's able to promptly make sound decisions in the face of multiple options, then you'll less likely fall into the paralysis or stress that causes most people to procrastinate.

The paradox of choice tends to impact things negatively because once people become overwhelmed with too many options, one of two things tends to happen.

One, after making a choice, you may still constantly think about the other options that you didn't choose. For instance, after buying a painting, you may still fixate on imagining how great the other paintings you didn't buy would look in place of the one you bought. So you're never really satisfied with the choices you make because a part of you remains preoccupied with thoughts of all the other options you missed out on by making a choice. It is the ultimate case of buyer's remorse.

Two, having too many options can subject you to a very difficult time deciding, such that you become paralyzed from making a decision and from doing anything at all. In philosophy, this is illustrated by the paradox of Buridan's ass (quite literally, donkey). Popularized by philosopher Jean Buridan, this paradox tells of a hungry donkey standing between two identical piles of hay. The donkey always chooses the hay closer to him, but this time both piles are of equal distance away. Unable to choose between the two piles, the donkey starves to death.

Applied to the mechanisms of work and productivity, the paradox of choice thus ultimately leads you to procrastinate, as you delay making a decision or starting on a task in an attempt to avoid the overwhelming pressure you feel from having so many options. The availability of options creates the illusion of greater personal responsibility to make not only the right choice, but the best one.

To beat the paradox of choice, the key is to set rules and restraints upon yourself. You'll need to find a way to see things in black and white, because gray areas are fertile grounds that breed overthinking and procrastination. That spectrum of gray is likely to see you get stuck and agonize over which shade of gray is the best choice until you get tired of the uncertainty, lose motivation, and end up being paralyzed from making any choice and acting at all. When Buridan's donkey saw shades of gray instead of one defined path to one defined dish of food, he faltered and ultimately starved to death.

To avoid falling into that trap, use the following strategies.

Focus on one factor and willfully ignore everything else. Every option is sure to offer its own pros and cons, and deciding among numerous options is not merely a matter of tabulating which has the most pros and the least cons. Rather, making a choice depends heavily on what you really care about, which often boils down to only one or two critical factors. So instead of having to deal with countless criteria that can overwhelm you from making a choice, focus only on one or two vital factors and ignore the rest. That way, you have a clearer idea about which option is best for you, and you can select it faster, too.

Suppose you need to buy a new microwave and have multiple models lined up in front of you, each with its own set of features and unique innovations. If you don't know which factors you want to focus on, it's easy to get confused by all the bells and whistles that such a large selection offers.

So to make it easier for you to make a choice that's really suited to your needs, decide beforehand on one or two specific features you want to mainly base your choice on—say, size (i.e., must fit your kitchen space) and sensor cooking. With just these two features in mind, you get to eliminate a lot of other models that don't fit the bill, thus effectively narrowing down your choices to make it easier for you to select the right one.

Set a time limit on making a decision. Commit to making a decision within, say, two minutes tops. Whatever decision you arrive at by the end of two minutes, stick with it no matter what. This defeats the paradox of choice by putting a cap on the amount of time you spend agonizing over which decision to make. It saves you from suffering the negative consequences of letting things pass you by and spurs you into the action necessary to realize your goals.

For example, imagine you're in charge of choosing and facilitating the venue for your upcoming gala but you're torn between Venue A and Venue B. You've put off making reservations for weeks now simply because you can't decide which venue would be the better choice. To save yourself from wasting any more time procrastinating, set two minutes for you to come up with a decision and pledge to stick with it.

You may go back and forth between the two venues within those two minutes, but once the time is up, whatever venue you settle on should be the one you go for—say, Venue A. To strengthen this strategy (no backsies!), make sure to call and make reservations for Venue A by the end of the two minutes.

Immediately choose a default option and stick with it if no better alternative comes up. Once you've selected one option as the default, you can set a short amount of time to try to find alternatives and weigh them against your default choice. If none of the alternatives measure up to your default, then you just revert to that default choice. That way, you're ensured of having already made a decision beforehand, which you can simply follow through with once it's time to act.

The fact that you've chosen a default already constitutes a choice in itself, one that you'll most likely be inclined to stick with and follow through on.

For example, again imagine you're in charge of choosing the venue for your upcoming gala, but you're so torn between Venue A and Venue B that you've put off facilitating the task altogether.

To save yourself from further procrastinating, you may set Venue A as your default choice, then allow three days for you to continue searching for other alternatives or to continue comparing the pros and cons between Venue A and Venue B. If by the end of the third day you find yourself either unconvinced by the other options or so convinced by all of them you're now confused, then just revert to your default choice of Venue A.

That way, you can start moving on with the rest of your event planning instead of getting stuck and procrastinating because you can't make a choice. Training your mind to select a default option preps it to be more inclined toward active decision-making rather than toward the passivity and paralysis that breeds procrastination habits.

Finally, strive to satisfice your desires more often than not. The word *satisfice* is a combination of the words *satisfy* and *suffice*. It's a term that Herbert Simon coined in the 1950s, and it represents what we should shoot for rather than something that is guaranteed to optimize and maximize our happiness.

Generally, people can be split into those two categories: those who seek to satisfice a decision and those who seek to maximize a decision.

Let's suppose that you are shopping for a new bike. The maximizer would devote hours to researching their decision and evaluating as many options as possible.

They would want to get the best one possible for their purposes and want to leave no stone unturned. They want 100% satisfaction despite the law of diminishing returns and the Pareto principle, which would warn against such measures.

By contrast, the satisficer is just shooting to be satisfied and is looking for an option that suffices for their purposes. They want something that works well enough to make them satisfied and pleased but not overjoyed or ecstatic. They aim for *good enough* and stop once they find that.

These are very different scales, and for this reason, studies have shown that satisficers tend to be happier with their decisions while maximizers tend to keep agonizing and thinking about greener pastures after their decisions.

Maximization represents a conundrum in our modern age, because while it is more possible now than at any other point in human history to get exactly what you want, there is also the paradox of choice, which makes it impossible to be satisfied. On a practical matter, there are few decisions where we should strive to maximize our value. Therefore, put forth proportional effort and just make a choice already.

Most of the time, you simply want something that is reliable and works. Suppose you are in a grocery store and you are trying to pick out the type of peanut butter you want. What should you shoot for here? Satisficing or maximizing? The same type of thinking should apply to 99% of our daily decisions.

Otherwise, we are constantly overwhelmed and waste our mental bandwidth where there are diminishing returns. Whatever net benefit the most optimal type of peanut butter brings to your life is likely not worth the extra effort it took to find it.

Motivation Follows Action

Another mindset to embrace in the battle against procrastination is the way in which true motivation and the appetite for productivity appears. Most of the time, whatever the real reason is, we end up telling ourselves that if we aren't in the mood (I don't *feel* like it), then it's not getting done.

Look, it would be five-million times easier to achieve our goals if we all knew how to motivate ourselves 100% of the time. It would be like pressing a magical button that jolts us out of bed and into work. Whenever our energy is faltering, we could just press the button again, and we'd be injected with another dose of that good stuff and be correspondingly productive. The closest legal thing we have to this is coffee, but even that has waning effects.

It's easier to feel motivated when you like a project or when you're doing something you are genuinely passionate about. But let's be realistic—there are days when just the mere act of leaving your bed is a challenge and a huge accomplishment. For most of us, we don't enjoy what we do enough to feel motivated by it. An artist may be inspired and motivated to bring her visions into reality, but for the rest of us? We're really just trying to scrape together enough willpower to get us through our days. This is all to clarify motivation's role in taking action and getting started.

Whatever your goals, motivation plays an important role and can spell the difference between success and failure. It's one of the most important ingredients to influence your drive and ambition, but we're thinking about it *all wrong*.

When we think about motivation, we want something that will light a spark in us and make us jump up from the couch and deeply into our tasks. We want *motivation that causes action*. There are a few problems with this, namely the fact that you're probably looking for something that doesn't exist, and that's going to keep you waiting on the sidelines, out of action and out of the race. This type of motivation, if you ever find it, is highly unreliable. If you feel that you need motivation that causes action, you are doing it wrong.

For instance, a writer who feels they are unable to write without some form of motivation or inspiration is going to stare at a blank page for hours. End of story.

The truth is, you should plan for life *without* a motivating kick-start. Seeking that motivation creates a prerequisite and additional barrier to action. Get into the habit of proceeding without it. And surprisingly, this is where you'll find what you were seeking. *Action leads to motivation*, more motivation, and eventually momentum.

The more you work for something, the more meaningful it becomes to you. Your own actions will be your fuel to move forward. After you've taken your first step and have seen progress from your efforts, motivation will come easier and more naturally, as will inspiration and discipline. You'll fall into a groove, and suddenly, you'll be in your work mood/mode. The first step will always be the hardest step, but the second step won't be.

For repetition's sake, forget motivation; get started, and you'll *become* motivated. Taking the first step is tough, but consider that aside from motivation, just getting started gives you many other things.

For instance, confidence also follows action. After all, how do you expect to be confident about something when you haven't even tried? A taste of action tells you that everything will be okay and you have nothing to fear. This is confidence rooted in firsthand experience, which is easier to find as opposed to false confidence that you get from trying to convince yourself before the fact that you can do it.

Public speaking is almost always a scary proposition. Consider how you might try to find confidence that causes action: you would tell yourself it will all be fine, imagine the audience in their underwear, and remind yourself of your hours of rehearsal. Now consider how you might find confidence after getting started—how action can cause confidence. "I did it and it was fine" is an easier argument to make versus "I haven't done it yet, but I think it will be fine."

The most important takeaway here is to not wait until you are 100% ready before you take the first step or that motivation is a necessary part of your process. It will probably never feel like you're completely ready. But starting down the road will motivate you more than anything else will before the fact, so allow your actions to motivate you and build confidence. Change your expectations regarding motivation, and remove the self-imposed requirements you have for yourself.

As a member of the human race, the tendency for procrastination may be hardwired into your limbic system, but that doesn't mean you should forever be a slave to your own primitive drives and impulses. Building these mindsets will turn you into an individual in better control of those drives and impulses so you can beat the lure of procrastination.

Takeaways:

- Procrastination may be a reflection of battling biological forces, and we can swing the battle in our favor if we use some of the mindset tactics in this chapter. Fear is an understated underlying cause of procrastination.
- The first such tactic is to understand how Newton's three laws of motion can apply to procrastination. Viewing your productivity (or lack thereof) as an equation is helpful because it allows you to think through the variables present in your life and learn how to manipulate them. First, an object at rest tends to stay at rest, while an object in motion tends to stay in motion (the first step is

the hardest step). Next, the amount of work produced is a product of the focus and the force that is applied toward it (focus your efforts intentionally). Finally, for every action, there is an equal and opposite reaction (take inventory of the productive and unproductive forces present in your life).

- Another factor in procrastination is the paradox of choice, wherein choices and options are actually detrimental because they cause indecision and plague us with doubt. They might even cause us to act like Buridan's donkey and proverbially starve to death between two dishes of food. To combat this, get into the habit of setting a time limit on your decisions, making matters black and white, aiming to become satisficed, and immediately picking a default option.

- Finally, understand that motivation and the mood to stop procrastinating is not something that appears spontaneously. It may never appear... *before* the fact.

But after you get started, it will almost always appear. Motivation *follows* action, yet most of us are seeking motivation that *creates* action. We are doing it backward and just need to get started to feel better, more often than not.

Chapter 4: Psychological Tactics

"Procrastination is the grave in which opportunity is buried."
—Anonymous

How do you get a machine to work?

You need to plug it into an energy source and push the right buttons. Now, getting yourself to work wouldn't be quite as simple as that, but in a way, you also have "energy sources" you can plug into and psychological "buttons" you can push to get yourself to be more productive and avoid procrastinating. If you know where to tap the energy to power yourself through tasks and which buttons to push—or avoid pushing—to get yourself to work, then you'll be able to beat procrastination and be well on your way to achieving your goals.

This chapter will introduce you to three psychological tactics that'll have you push just the right buttons in your own psyche so you can get yourself up and running as you set about accomplishing your tasks. Here are these four tactics: (1) don't rely on your mood, (2) deal with omission bias, (3) visualize your future self, and (4) use the if-then technique.

No One Simply "Feels Like it"

How many times have you put off a task just because you're "not yet in the mood" to work on it or because you "don't feel like working"? What's your record for the length of time you've waited to "feel the right moment to start" before you actually set about on a task?

This sounds suspiciously like how the last chapter left off, about action being what creates motivation. Instead of waiting for your mood to spark you into action, act first in order to spark your mood into a motivated, all-systems-go mode.

Start operating under the notion that the right action inspires the right mood, instead of the other way around. For example, whether or not you feel in the mood to research that project you're supposed to do, sit yourself down and start browsing a page on the subject. Soon enough, you'll find yourself gaining more and more momentum, and you'll feel more and more motivated to keep with the task.

No matter what mood you're in—happy or cranky, excited or bored, calm or edgy—just start. You know all this, and now we go beyond the simple assertion that action is what matters. The question still remains: how do we get to that point? We can logically know that we are acting against our own interests but still remain stuck to the couch.

Researchers have designed a playbook of strategies to help you get there. The added benefit to mastering this playbook is that it will not only help you take action no matter what mood you're in, but also equip you with strategies to repair your mood in general. So whether it's your intention to kick the procrastination bug out of your system or to simply convert negative feelings into positive ones, practice the two psychological tricks described below to experience a mood boost whenever you need one.

First, set a low threshold for getting started. As advised by Dr. Timothy Pychyl, a leading researcher in the field of procrastination, making the threshold for getting started relatively low can trick your mind into getting motivated for a task. The low threshold suggests to you that the task is completely manageable, and anticipating that you'll easily get past the first hurdle of the task will help you boost positive emotions in relation to the work you need to do. By increasing the positive feelings you associate with a task, you'll be more likely to jump in on it. In fact, you want to make it so easy to start that it doesn't inconvenience you in the slightest and it's almost like you aren't doing anything at all. You may not be in a mood to do anything difficult, but something neutral might be possible.

Suppose you need to create a PowerPoint presentation of your company profile. To set a low threshold, decide to only work on just the titles of each slide, or even just pick a background design. Leave the actual details and content for later; it's not pertinent to your current threshold and goal of just getting started. Score an easy win and start to gain momentum that leads you away from the couch.

A low threshold doesn't only have to be with regard to the time commitment. It can also be in regard to the *quality* of what you're producing. Instead of trying to write 500 words a day, try to write 500 words of *crap*—lowering your standards will help you stop overthinking and simply get into action.

Creating a low threshold to get started touches upon one of the greatest obstacles—viewing a task as the larger end product. When something is so big and insurmountable, it feels pointless to do anything.

Thus, try to focus on the process rather than the product. While product pertains to the outcome of your efforts, process refers to the actions you take and the flow of time that passes as you work toward that outcome. The end goal will never change, but it's about how you view it.

If you've ever witnessed or heard how the Japanese conduct tea ceremonies—how every step of the ceremony has significance and is thus done with the utmost care and respect—you'll easily recognize what a focus on process rather than product looks like.

For the Japanese, tea ceremonies aren't done just so one can produce and fill their bellies with tea. Rather, the ceremonies are done for their own sake—the process itself has more significance than the product does. And when you focus on the process and dedicate your full attention to it, the product inevitably comes as a result of that process—the tea gets made and drank in the end.

Now, how does this relate to procrastination? When you need to do something, especially if it's a large task, it's easy to get overwhelmed by the pressure of having to deliver the product.

This pressure is usually enough for people to opt for procrastination instead of taking on that task. To avoid this, try to focus on the process of doing that task. What do you need to do in order to get the job done? Break things down into smaller tasks, then schedule these tasks to be done within chunks of time spread out over days or weeks. These smaller tasks are easier to swallow mentally, and the bite-sized portions relieve you of pressure by allowing you to focus just on one particular work block at a time, rather than allowing you to get intimidated by the idea of an overarching goal.

For example, suppose you need to devise a handbook intended for visitors who come by your company. The handbook is your product. Thinking about this product in its entirety—must include everything from company background, vision and mission, organizational chart, and safety reminders for visitors—can trigger overwhelming feelings of dread about having to undertake such a mammoth task.

So instead of focusing on the product (i.e., the entire handbook), focus on the process of creating that product section by section. Assign yourself only one section for a particular chunk of time—say, piecing together the organizational chart for this hour. Do the next section at another scheduled time, and so on, until you complete the entire thing.

Keep your eyes focused on what's in front of you and just complete your tasks. By focusing on a section-by-section approach, you get to ease into the process and feel that you're accomplishing things throughout instead of experiencing a sense of success only at the end of it.

Think of this strategy as similar to building a structure brick by brick. You'll be better motivated to start working and keep going when you know you just have a specific number of bricks to lay at a time, rather than expecting yourself to plop down a huge structure all at once.

Because you have no unrealistic expectations of yourself, you're also saved from having to feel an overwhelming amount of pressure to accomplish the impossible. You get to pace yourself well and don't feel guilty about "just laying 10 bricks for the day" because you're well aware of the fact that those "10 bricks" constitute enough work that'll still allow you to achieve your goal on time.

Second, forgive yourself for procrastinating.

One way that you get overpowered by procrastination is by letting yourself think that your past procrastination slip-ups are irredeemable and that they have done such irreparable damage that you might as well give up on trying to remedy the situation altogether. You feel guilty and blame yourself for being too weak to fight off procrastination, so you get discouraged trying to do the task any longer.

For instance, you may think that because you've procrastinated on doing that research project for the past hour, any attempt to start researching now is already a lost cause, so you decide to spend the rest of the evening just procrastinating. When you forgive yourself, you stop thinking in terms of lost causes, move past wallowing in self-pity, and move to the next phase, which is action.

Instead of wallowing in that bottomless pit of self-blame and guilt, resolve to forgive yourself for procrastinating and pick up the motivation to start anew once you recognize you've slipped up. As associate psychology professor Michael Wohl found in a 2010 study, university freshmen who forgave themselves for putting off studying for the first exam procrastinated less on the next exam. Forgiving yourself for procrastinating thus decreases the likelihood of you later procrastinating on your tasks. Instead of being problem-focused ("I can't believe I have so much to do!"), become solution-focused ("What steps do I take now?").

Someone with the problem-oriented mindset obsesses on the problem itself. They wonder what went wrong. They get upset that it keeps happening. They seek blame and responsibility for the problem, and the only answer they have for the problem is to "avoid it." They are unable to move past their negative feelings regarding a problem or obstacle.

To come up with a solution in this mindset, determine what your existing conditions are now (Point A) and how you eventually want them to turn out (Point B). By getting a clear understanding of each point and the gap between them, you'll get a much better sense of what you need to do.

Think of the problem in terms of checklists. You could make a list of everything that's going wrong. Alternatively, you could make a list that describes potential solutions. Only one of these checklists is actionable. The only actions you can derive from a list of problems are complaining and fixating on failure. With a list of actions, you have options you can immediately pursue. Only the action list has real value.

Out of Sight, Out of Mind

If we know procrastinating is bad for us, why do we still keep doing it? As previously discussed, biological explanations point to the roles of the lizard brain running wild with primitive drives and impulses and to the prefrontal cortex not being strong or skilled enough to get those drives and impulses under control.

But what about the psychological explanation for our proclivity for doing something that causes problems for us? What is it in our human psyche and cognitive processes that predisposes us to put off tasks until later, even when we know we should really be doing them now?

According to business site Harvard Business Review, we can chalk it up to what is known as *omission bias*. Omission bias is a cognitive distortion by which we fail to see the consequences of *not* doing something.

While it's easy for us to envision the consequences of committing something bad, it's harder for us to imagine the costs of omission. This is because when we perform or witness an action, we are primed to anticipate an effect that arises out of that action. We wait to see what happens afterward. But when there's no tangible action, our minds find no reason to try to see how that might change things for us.

We tend to just go about our lives not even thinking of omission as possibly having effects, precisely because we think there wasn't an action to cause any effects in the first place. Essentially, out of sight, out of mind.

For instance, it tends to be easier for us to picture how frequently eating a load of greasy fast food meals is going to risk our heart health, but it's harder for us to recognize how *not* exercising can place us at the same health risk. While we may actively avoid those oily take-out meals in an attempt to maintain a healthy lifestyle, we aren't as likely to start an exercise regimen to support that same goal. It just doesn't have the same psychological impact.

Omission bias is often at play when we procrastinate on tasks. See, procrastination is essentially an omission—it's the phenomenon of *not* doing our intended tasks. Owing to our bias against considering the pros and cons of not doing things, we tend to feel less alarmed by our procrastination tendencies, because technically, since we're not doing anything, our minds take that to mean we can't possibly be doing anything wrong.

Our minds reason, *"How can we be doing anything wrong if we're literally not doing anything?"* Such is the brilliant "logic" of our mind: bending reason to support our procrastination habits so we get to continue reaping short-term pleasures while remaining blind to the negative impacts of our inaction.

So how do you get out of the rut that omission bias creates for you? The answer starts with awareness. Once you're better aware of the gravity of consequences attached to not doing a task, you'll also be more motivated to start doing that task. Recognize how omission bias tends to operate in your life, how it has sabotaged your motivation to work on tasks in the past, and how it's likely to affect your future decisions and actions.

Proactively magnifying the negative effects of omission bias on your life is a powerful way to confront it and a key strategy to transition from procrastination to productivity. There may not be any immediate negative effects, but as you start to think outward from yourself and into the future, more and more will materialize. More than simple awareness is needed from time to time.

For example, say you've been putting off your task of reviewing and updating your company's current policies and procedures on chemical disposal. If you aren't aware of your own omission bias, you'll likely feel as if you're not really doing anything wrong, because there's a current system in place that's working anyway. However, you're conveniently ignoring the negative impact that *not* doing that task might carry, including health risks for everyone in the community.

Continuing to employ outdated chemical disposal methods may be poisoning your neighborhood's water supply or hazarding the health of all company employees, including your own. But without proactively imagining these negative effects of inaction, you'll be less likely to feel the urge to act. To remedy the situation, reconsider the negative consequences of not doing the task at hand and use it to motivate yourself to get working.

Visualize Your Future Self

Remember that the defining feature of procrastination isn't just the act of putting off tasks; it's the deliberate delaying of intended tasks, even while knowing full well that such delay will cause negative consequences in the future. Well, guess who suffers in that scenario? Procrastination isn't just about complacency or mere forgetfulness. It's more about hazarding the welfare of our future selves as we focus on gaining short-term pleasure at the cost of long-term benefits.

Dr. Pychyl from earlier suggests that you "time travel."

Don't worry: this book hasn't taken a turn to sci-fi-ville. Time travel here pertains to the practice of projecting yourself into the future as a way to anticipate how good you'd feel if you finish a task and how bad you'd feel if you don't. Vividly think about your future self and how they will feel. This strategy remedies the tendency to get so caught up in your present anxieties—or present pleasures—such that you fail to appreciate the relief and sense of fulfillment that comes once you accomplish a task and the horror that comes if you don't.

When you can associate immediate actions with longer-term consequences, suddenly you gain perspective on what you should or shouldn't be doing. Visualize your future and all the positive and negative consequences that arise from a small, immediate action. Use your imagination.

For example, if you're not feeling motivated to work on a speech you've been asked to do, picture yourself already up on that podium in the heat of the moment. How would it go if you went into it well-prepared? What kind of applause would you receive, and how many accolades might you garner afterward? How satisfying is the feeling of a job well done, especially if it was a challenge?

On the other hand, how might you sound if you failed to prepare for it well enough? How red would your face be if you were stumbling for words, and how much brow sweat would accumulate? How might a poor performance change people's perceptions of you? Soak in that feeling of anxiety and panic.

Now you have a very clear picture of what's at stake. Picture the pains and the triumphs and use them as a mental boost. Admittedly, the pains will probably be more motivating, but that's okay. In small doses, pushing yourself using fear is a necessary evil.

Other scientists have supported this notion. Research into chronic procrastination has unearthed an interesting discovery on what sets apart chronic procrastinators from the rest. We each have a way of transporting our mind into the future—we do it whenever we set goals, plan, or bring up positive affirmations.

Through these activities, we're able to connect with our future selves and visualize how we're going to transition from our present situation to that future vision. For chronic procrastinators, though, that vision of their future selves tends to be blurry, more abstract, and impersonal.

They often feel an emotional disconnect between who they are at the present and who they'll become in the future. Thus, they have a harder time delaying gratification. As they are more strongly in tune with the desires of their present selves and don't feel connected enough with their future selves to care about their welfare, chronic procrastinators thus more readily give in to the lure of short-term pleasures.

Rather than sacrifice present comfort for future rewards, they choose to revel in what feels good now because their vision tends to be more limited to the immediate moment. This is what psychology professor Dr. Fuschia Sirois calls *temporal myopia* (more easily thought of as nearsightedness with regards to time)—a key quality that may largely underlie chronic procrastination.

To further clarify the phenomenon of how our perception of time can influence the way we make decisions, Hal Hershfield, a professor of marketing at UCLA's Anderson School of Management, conducted experiments. Using virtual reality,

Hershfield had people interact with their future self.

The results of his experiments revealed that people who interacted with their future selves were more likely to be concerned about both their present and future selves, and they also tended to act favorably in consideration of their future selves. For instance, they were much more likely to put money in a fake, experiment-based retirement account for the benefit of the future self they interacted with.

What did Hershfield's studies show us? The better we're able to visualize and interact with our future self, the better we get at taking good care of it. This is because by visualizing and connecting with our future self, we feel the reality of the upcoming circumstances and recognize how the actions of our present self are bound to create a real impact on our future self.

By practicing visualization, we start to see how procrastinating now may be good for our present self but disastrous for our future self. As we empathize with the fate of our future self and the kind of life it will have to live through if we keep the habit of procrastination up (e.g., sleepless nights trying to get caught up with work, turning in haphazardly done output, having to deal with career failures), we begin to feel motivated to change our present ways to be more productive.

So the next time you're feeling drawn to procrastinate, think of your future self. Visualize every little step and reaction your future self would make in both situations. Getting a taste of the two alternate lives your future self might experience will increase your motivation to act toward realizing your success rather than the failure.

As you come to appreciate the beauty of a success scenario, visualize what the completed task looks like and trace your way back—that is, outline the specific tasks you need to perform to get to that vision of your future self proudly completing the task at hand and reaping its rewards.

Keeping your future self in mind will serve as a reminder both of the positive consequences of beating procrastination and of the negative impacts of failing to fight the urge to delay your intended tasks.

The If-Then Technique

The final technique dealing with your mindset is the *if-then technique*. This is also sometimes known as an *implementation intention*—in other words, making your intention easy to implement. The *if* portion corresponds to the cue, while the *then* portion corresponds to the routine.

If-then statements take the following form: if X happens, then I will do Y. That's it. This helps you avoid procrastination because you never deal with it in the heat of the moment. You make the decision beforehand. When actions are chained and given forethought, they tend to happen more often than not.

As a quick example, *if* it is 3:00 p.m. on Sunday, *then* you will call your mother. *If* it is 3:00 p.m., *then* you will drink two liters of water. *If* you have just taken a break, *then* you will take care of some chores. These are examples of when you use if-then to accomplish a specific goal—the first type of use. X can be whatever event, time, or occurrence you choose that happens on a daily basis, and Y is the specific action that you will take.

The if-then statement simply takes your desired goals out of the ether and ties them to concrete moments in your day. A goal to eat healthier or get started on work has a set prescription because it is tied to a daily occurrence that is unavoidable. Instead of generalities, you get a time and place for when to act.

It seems simplistic, and it is, but it has been shown that you are two to three times more likely to succeed if you use an if-then plan than if you don't. In one study, 91% of people who used an if-then plan stuck to an exercise program versus 39% of non-planners. Peter Gollwitzer, the NYU psychologist who first articulated the power of if-then planning, recently reviewed results from 94 studies that used the technique and found significantly higher success rates for just about every goal you can think of, from using public transportation more frequently to avoiding stereotypical and prejudicial thoughts.

Let's say your significant other has been giving you a hard time about forgetting to text to inform them that you will be working late and not make dinner. So you make an if-then plan: if it is 6:00 p.m. and I'm at work, then I will text my significant other. Now the situation "6:00 p.m. at work" is wired in your brain directly to the action "text my sugar bear."

Then the situation or cue "6:00 p.m. at work" becomes highly activated. Below your awareness, your brain starts scanning the environment, searching for the situation in the "if" part of your plan. Once the "if" part of your plan happens, the "then" part follows *automatically*. You don't *have* to consciously monitor your goal, which means your plans get carried out even when you are preoccupied.

The best part is that by detecting situations and directing behavior without conscious effort, if-then plans are far less taxing and require less willpower than mere resolutions. They enable us to conserve our self-discipline for when it's really needed and compensate for it when we don't have enough. Armed with if-thens, you can tell your fickle friend willpower that this year, you really won't be needing him.

All of these methods help focus on the minute but powerful triggers that lead us into the personal infractions we're trying to eliminate, and they help defray the residual personal reactions that arise from forcing change in our lives. Best of all, they don't rely on sweeping or exhaustive changes to who we are—they make our brains and natural impulses work *for* us instead of going to sleep on the job.

Once again, deciding exactly how you'll react to circumstances regarding your goal creates a link in your brain between the situation or cue (if) and the behavior that should follow (then). And as we know, everything good that we want happens in our brain.

Learn to push the right psychological "buttons" to rid yourself of procrastination and become a more productive individual. As you master the art of repairing your mood, confronting your omission bias, and visualizing your future self, you'll have less and less trouble starting up. Yes, as a human being with your own set of drives and impulses, you may never get yourself to work as simply as you can turn a machine on.

But with the right psychological tactics, you can achieve a mastery of yourself well enough to be able to manage those drives and impulses and steer yourself toward productivity and maximum efficiency.

Takeaways:

- Sometimes it's necessary to trick ourselves into doing what we don't want to. In fact, that's a primary aspect of improving and practicing anything. We are momentarily seduced by the benefit or end result to the point where we can grin and bear the present pain.
- Many of us think we can only work when we are in the mood for it or when inspiration strikes us. That is a losing battle. Don't rely on your mood to get you where you want to go. Instead, think the opposite way: once you begin action, your mood will follow. To get to action quicker, think in terms of low thresholds to get started, as well as focusing only on the process and not the end product.

Also, forgive yourself for procrastinating, and instead of thinking about the problem, think about the possible checklist of solutions.

- Understand and tame omission bias. This is when you realize that it's easy to feel the impact of doing something but not the impact of skipping something. This is about more than awareness; you can battle omission bias with proactive visualization of the bad future you are creating. That will kick you into gear.

- Visualize your future self. Most of us suffer from *temporal myopia,* which is when you are nearsighted with regards to time. But your everyday actions can lead you to vastly different futures. Think about your future self; when you can effectively visualize the personal consequences of your actions (positive and negative) in excruciating detail, you are more aware of what you need to do and more impacted by it.

- Finally, use if-then statements. These make procrastination difficult because the decisions are made beforehand. If a certain daily event occurs, then you will start working in some aspect. When behaviors are chained together and tied to concrete milestones, they become easier.

Chapter 5: Strategic Planning

"You don't have to see the whole staircase, just take the first step."
—Martin Luther King, Jr.

When it comes to beating procrastination, half the battle is getting a good strategy in place. If you plan your tasks well and set up your workload strategically, you can strip away the chances of slipping into procrastination. No more delaying the start of a project, straying off task, or getting tempted into engaging in mindless, unimportant activities—rather, you can structure things to set yourself up for productivity, efficiency, and achievement.

This chapter will teach you four strategic planning tactics to preempt procrastination before it even begins: (1) use the STING method, (2) manipulate variables in the "procrastination equation," (3) use temptation bundling, and (4) use the Eisenhower matrix.

Think STING

The STING method represents an acronym for five strategies you can implement in order to prevent procrastination. It stands for select one task (S), time yourself (T), ignore everything else (I), no breaks (N), and give yourself a reward (G). For those of us who need to be reined in, a strict guideline can be helpful.

S - Select one task. In order to avert procrastination, focus is the name of the game. And when there is more than one task in front of you, your focus will tend to be divided as well. Instead of immediately starting on a task, you'll be led to ask yourself, *"Should I do Task A, Task B, or Task C first? How about I find a way to do them all at once? Or how about I put off doing any of them at all?"*

Being overwhelmed by numerous tasks in front of you can be a precursor to procrastination, as having to make a decision paralyzes you from taking action. Also, having a large goal with no clear, smaller subtasks you can easily work on can be off-putting. Not knowing how or where to start, you may instead succumb to procrastination and opt for other enjoyable activities instead.

To remedy the situation, select a single, small task on which you should focus at a particular time. With a clear course of action laid out in front of you, you'll be less likely to try to escape an overwhelming or confusing situation by procrastination.

T - Time yourself. One notion that often breeds procrastination is the thought of having to work on a task for endless, punishing hours. With such a gloomy forecast of how your life might look in the near future if you jump into the task at hand, you'll be likely to opt for delaying the task instead. In other words, when you can't see light at the end of the tunnel, it's a normal response for you to avoid entering that tunnel in the first place—that is, to procrastinate. Because what's the point of troubling yourself with a task when you can't see an end to it anyway?

Timing yourself is a good strategy to counter the threat of procrastination in this situation. Timing yourself means setting a predetermined amount of time you'll be spending on a particular task. Give yourself, say, one hour to work on that business proposal, and promise to stop once the hour is up, regardless of whether you've finished the task.

That way, you'll be more motivated to start working on it, because you can see the "light at the end of the tunnel"—a respite from the labor at the end of the hour. Moreover, you'll be better driven to work more efficiently because you know you only have so much time to spend on that task. You'll want to make each minute count, as the countdown ignites in you a sense of urgency and competition against the clock (or yourself), pushing you to move while the time still allows it.

I - Ignore everything else. As you're doing the task in the moment, focus only on that task and ignore everything else. This is easier to do when you've selected only one task and have timed yourself, as these first two strategies allow you to narrow down your focus and reassure you that you can bother with other tasks, or indulge in distractions, as soon as the time you've set is up.

In the meantime, you need to focus solely on the task you've selected and put your blinders on, ignoring everything else unrelated to the task at hand. It's understandably hard to be able to pull that off without slipping, especially when you're used to indulging in the distractions all around you. However, the moment you do manage to completely ignore everything else and simply focus on the task, you will experience an incredible clarity and sense of self-assurance.

You discover that you do have it in you to stand your ground as you ignore extraneous stuff and that the world didn't end when you chose to disregard all the distractions around you. Those distractions are not urgent, nor are they important, so they only serve to throw you off task.

For example, if you've committed to accomplishing an activity report within the next hour, focus solely on that and ignore everything else—whether it's thoughts about the next thing on your to-do list or environmental distractors such as your mobile phone, your email alerts, and your chatty colleague. Ignoring these shields you from the extraneous stuff that detracts you from your purpose and thus prevents you from procrastinating.

N - No breaks. Within the time frame you've set for focusing on a task, make sure you refrain from taking breaks. Breaks are necessary to revive your energy levels and recharge your mental stamina, but they shouldn't be taken willy-nilly. If you've planned your schedule effectively, you should already have scheduled breaks at appropriate times throughout the day, so any other breaks in the midst of ongoing workhours are unwarranted.

While scheduled breaks keep you on track by being strategic, reenergizing methods of self-reinforcement, unscheduled breaks derail you from your goal, as they offer you opportunities to procrastinate by making you feel as if you've got "free time."

Taking unscheduled breaks is a surefire way to fall into the procrastination trap. You may rationalize that you're only getting a cup of coffee to keep yourself alert, but in reality, you're just trying to avoid having to work on a task at your desk. You start off by getting that cup of coffee, but the next thing you know, you're already happily chattering away at the next cubicle or enjoying YouTube binge-watching in a corner. Once you allow yourself unplanned breaks, you'll be more likely to find yourself captive to procrastination. So to prevent procrastination, commit to having no random breaks instead.

G - Give yourself a reward. Once you're done with a task, reward yourself. Indulge in a favorite snack, treat yourself to a movie, or snuggle down to a good nap. This tactic deters procrastination because it pulls you forward into starting and completing a task by promising something pleasurable at the end. Remember that humans are creatures hardwired to avoid pain and pursue pleasure.

While this same mechanism can lure you into procrastination, it can also be hacked to keep you away from procrastination— and that is by promising to give yourself a reward upon achieving your goal on time. That way, you're giving yourself an extra incentive for accomplishing the task, and the anticipation of that reward will motivate you to power through the work needed to attain it.

Used together in sequence, STING creates a pod of undisturbed time and effort for you to get things done. It's entirely possible to string a few of these pods together in a day, with scheduled breaks in between.

Manipulate the "Procrastination Equation"

Yes, you read that right—someone has formulated an equation of procrastination, one that elegantly works out the interaction of variables that make procrastination more likely to occur.

That someone is Piers Steel, a leading researcher on procrastination. While Stephen Guise applied Newton's three laws of motion to the mechanisms of productivity, Steel distilled and synthesized 691 studies on the subject to come up with a comprehensive, evidence-based equation that explains motivation and procrastination.

Known as the "procrastination equation," Steel drew up the formula as follows:

$$Motivation = \frac{Expectancy \times Value}{Impulsiveness \times Delay}$$

In the equation, motivation pertains to your drive to do your intended task. The higher your motivation, the less likely you're going to procrastinate. The lower your motivation, the more likely you're going to procrastinate.

As shown in the equation, your level of motivation depends on four variables: (1) expectancy, (2) value, (3) impulsiveness, and (4) delay.

Expectancy refers to your expectation of succeeding at the task. For example, if you need to deliver a sales presentation, expectancy pertains to how much you expect the presentation to be a success, as evidenced by your client buying your product or simply by your effective delivery of the presentation. Note that the expectancy variable is in the numerator of the equation. This means that the higher your expectancy of success, the more motivated you're going to be to work on your task.

Value pertains to the importance, worth, or pleasantness of the task to you. How much does your intended task matter to you? How much do you like doing that task? Your answers to these questions speak of the value you attach to the task. If the sales presentation you're about to do matters very much to you, and/or you actually like working on a sales presentation, then you're more likely to be motivated to get going on it.

Like the expectancy variable, the value variable is also in the numerator of the equation, which means the more you value the task, the greater your motivation for doing it is.

Now let's talk about the two variables in the denominator of the equation: impulsiveness and delay.

Impulsiveness refers to your tendency to act on your impulses immediately, without first thinking through their consequences.

The more impulsive you are, the more likely you tend to follow your desires and urges at the drop of a hat. From this description, you can imagine just how being impulsive is related to procrastinating.

For example, let's say that in the middle of preparing for your sales presentation, you feel the urge to check on your social media accounts. If you have an impulsive personality, you'll feel strongly compelled to act on that urge, thus lowering your motivation to focus on the task and leading you to procrastinate instead. This is the reason why impulsiveness is in the denominator of the procrastination equation. Its relationship with motivation is inverse: the more impulsive you are, the less motivated you'll be to work on your intended task.

Finally, there's the variable called delay.

Delay pertains to the interval of time between your completion of a task and your receipt of the reward for doing so. For instance, suppose you've been told that the cash incentive for successfully delivering your sales presentation wouldn't be given to you until your retirement. How would you feel about working on that presentation now?

Such a long delay between your task completion and its reward is likely to decrease your motivation for working on it. The longer you expect to wait for the payoff, the more difficult it is for you to push yourself to get going on the task. This is why the delay variable is in the denominator of the equation. Like impulsiveness, its relationship with motivation is inverse: the greater the delay of the reward, the lesser motivation you'll feel to work on the task.

In summary, here is what's at work when it comes to procrastination: the more you expect to succeed and the more you value a task, the more you're motivated to work on it, and therefore, the less likely you're going to procrastinate. On the other hand, the more impulsive you are and the more delayed the payoff for the task is, the less you're motivated to work, and therefore, the more likely it is that you're going to procrastinate.

And now to answer the million-dollar question: how do you manipulate those variables to beat procrastination?

The beauty of arranging the components of procrastination as variables in a mathematical equation is that you get to clearly see which components you need to increase and which you need to decrease. Let's take a look at the general equation again:

$$Motivation = \frac{Expectancy \times Va}{Impulsiveness \times D}$$

Given the equation, the formula for increasing motivation—and therefore decreasing procrastination—is simple: increase the numerators (expectancy and value) and decrease the denominators (impulsiveness and delay).

You may choose to implement a combination of those techniques to increase your motivation, depending on what best applies to your situation.

For example, if you already have high expectations of success and attach a high value to the task but tend to be highly impulsive and easily give in to temptations, then you know you've got to work on decreasing the impulsiveness variable—so maybe try to eliminate distractions in your environment and practice being more thoughtful rather than being overly reactive.

If you aren't impulsive but tend to procrastinate because you lack self-confidence and expect failure, then work on increasing your expectancy for success by working to discover your strengths and learning how to apply them to succeed in your task.

Let's consider how manipulating the procrastination equation would look when applied to our earlier scenario of being tasked to deliver a sales presentation. Remember that given the variables in the procrastination equation—expectancy, value, impulsiveness, and delay—there are at least four ways you can go about increasing your motivation to work on this task.

First, increase your expectancy of success. Put simply, you need to be more optimistic. Think positive! Concrete strategies to help you do so include watching motivational videos, calling to mind situations in the past in which you've succeeded, and engaging in visualization.

Believe in your capacity to do the presentation well and visualize a scene in which your audience is interested and captivated by your presentation and your client reacts positively to your pitch. To prevent this visualization from being just a daydream, though, researchers suggest employing a technique called mental contrasting.

After imagining your presentation going well, mentally contrast that with the actual situation you're in right now. How much work have you really done at this point to be able to realize that vision? This technique is effective at jumpstarting planning and action, driving you to move yourself from your current situation to a successful outcome.

Second, increase the value of the task to you. If doing a sales presentation is something you already highly value because you find it worthwhile or enjoyable, then you don't need to do much more other than continually remind yourself of why it's valuable to you. But if doing the presentation is something you dislike or find meaningless, then your task is to find an aspect of it you could like or to create meaning in the task.

The art of self-motivation has a lot to do with managing your own perceptions. To increase task value, you may consider how doing that sales presentation well could have repercussions on your career progression and, ultimately, your quality of life. Reframe the task not as an end in itself but as a means to an end you value, and you'll find yourself better motivated to get going on it.

Third, decrease your level of impulsiveness. While some people tend to be inherently more impulsive than others, everyone can implement strategies to decrease their overall impulsiveness.

These strategies will need you to modify and structure your environment in such a way that you'll have fewer opportunities to act on your impulses. Suggested by Steel, this approach needs you to "throw away the key." For instance, while working on your sales presentation, close all other tabs on your computer that may tempt you to procrastinate (e.g., YouTube, Facebook, Instagram pages). Don't work in front of the TV.

Eat a good meal before sitting down to work so that you won't be tempted to get up for snack time again while you're working.

Finally, decrease the delay of the reward after task completion. While this variable is less likely to be in your control than the other components (e.g., you're usually not the one who has a say on when you're going to get compensated), there are still ways you can tweak this variable to your advantage. For instance, break down the task into smaller subtasks and reward yourself for completing each of those subtasks.

That way, you can keep feeding your motivation with little reinforcements throughout the process of working on that larger task. Think of it as continuing to feed the fire with small sticks in order to keep it burning. In making your presentation, for instance, reward yourself with a nice meal or a movie when you complete a subtask, such as completing the presentation outline.

By knowing how to steer each of the equation variables in just the right direction, you'll have the power to increase your motivation level and decrease your procrastination habits as you please.

Temptation Bundling

Temptation bundling is the final way to kill procrastination and increase productivity by combining present and future selves and their conflicting needs.

Conceived by behavioral scientist Katy Milkman at the University of Pennsylvania, temptation bundling is a way to blend both future and present self needs by making future rewards more immediate. You give yourself instant gratification in the present while also achieving goals that benefit your future self in the long-term. In our context, this is satisfying both the limbic system *and* the prefrontal cortex simultaneously.

It's simpler than it sounds.

If your goal is to satisfy the two versions of yourself (current and future), think about what that would require. Future self wants you to buckle down and take care of business so they are in a good position—or at least not suffering from your neglect. However, current self wants to engage in hedonism and enjoy the present moment. Think eating Twinkies while working out, working out while watching TV, or doing work while soaking your feet in a salt bath—these are examples of ways to make the long-term feel good at the present moment, and this is the essence of temptation bundling.

Bundle a temptation (current pleasure) with an unpleasurable activity (something you would otherwise procrastinate and that your future self would be pleased to avoid), and you get the best of both worlds.

There is no need to suffer in the present to get something done for your future self; if you do suffer, then you will lose all motivation and procrastinate. So find ways to bundle your temptations with your long-term goals. In other words, pair your obligations with instantaneous rewards.

Milkman found that up to 51% of her study participants were willing to exercise with temptation bundling. It is an effective means to correct procrastination habits. You should make a list with two columns, one side being your guilty pleasures or temptations and the other side being things you need to do for your future self. Then figure out creative ways to link the two conflicting columns in harmony.

Suppose you like chocolate, surfing, soccer, and running. But work, homework, and piano lessons stand in your way.

Chocolate	Homework
Surfing	Work
Soccer	Piano Lessons

How might you combine things to make the unpleasurable more tolerable? There are at least nine combinations of these elements and nine different ways you can bundle temptations. How might you combine chocolate with homework, soccer with work, and surfing with piano lessons? It doesn't take long to imagine how you can bribe yourself into doing exactly what you need to do. Hopefully, the temptation you seek doesn't directly undo the effects of your work, such as rewarding yourself with a donut for going to the gym, but sometimes it's worthwhile to take two steps forward and one step backward.

All you're doing is bribing yourself strategically. It's simple and can even work the opposite way in doling out small punishments in the absence of action—though that's not my particular cup of tea. That said, negativity does tend to be a more powerful motivating factor. For instance, you might pair a lack of finishing homework with a lack of chocolate or deprival of surfing the next day.

The Eisenhower Matrix

A final way we can plan against procrastination is to understand what we should actually be doing at the current moment.

Many things will appear to be emergencies that should be handled as soon as humanly possible, and horrible consequences will follow if you don't personally act. Almost all of these are false alarms and thus keep you from moving forward.

The mistake is thinking of "important" and "urgent" as synonymous and not realizing the huge gulf of difference between the two terms and how you should prioritize them. We spend far too much time on *urgent* tasks when we should be focusing on *important* tasks.

Important task: These contribute directly to our short-term or long-term goals. They are absolutely imperative to our work, responsibilities, or lives. They cannot be skipped and should be prioritized. They may not need to be done immediately and thus don't appear to be important. This makes it easy to fall into the trap of ignoring the important for the urgent. But they are what truly impact your various bottom lines, and serious negative repercussions would follow from skipping them.

Urgent task: These simply demand immediacy and speed, and they usually come from other people. Of course, this naturally creates a reaction on your end that can make us forget what's important. They *can* overlap with an important task, but they can also just demand your immediate attention without deserving it. These are usually smaller and easier to complete, so often we turn to them out of procrastination, and it allows us to feel quasi-productive even though we've ignored what we *really* need to be doing. Many urgent tasks can be delayed, delegated, or flat-out ignored.

As a quick example, if you are an author under a tight deadline, an *important* task for you would be to continue writing your book. You need to hit 5,000 words a day for the next two weeks or else you are going to be eating bread and oatmeal. This would qualify as a priority.

An *urgent* task would be dealing with that annoying "check engine" light that keeps flickering on and off in your car. Your car can probably survive a few more trips, and even though the light winking can be seductive, you need to resist it, because this is urgent masquerading as important.

Typically, you'll find that an important activity or project might not have that many urgent tasks connected with it. This tends to cause confusion of priorities. Luckily, there is a tried and true method of distinguishing between urgent and important, and the method draws its name from one of the most famous American presidents, Dwight D. Eisenhower. It's called the Eisenhower matrix, and it will help you prioritize and identify what you really need to be juggling at the moment.

Eisenhower developed a system that helped him sort his activities and demands into matters that were most important and helped him identify the most vital processes to serve those important elements. In other words, important versus urgent.

Eisenhower's matrix is easy for anyone to employ and goes a long way toward improving efficiency and accomplishment. The template is a simple two-by-two grid divided between "important" goals and "urgent" tasks, as seen below.

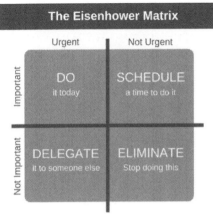

The Eisenhower Matrix

	Urgent	Not Urgent
Important	DO it today	SCHEDULE a time to do it
Not Important	DELEGATE it to someone else	ELIMINATE Stop doing this

www.expertprogrammanagement.com

Important tasks. The top row of the matrix represents the most important obligations or responsibilities one has in their life. These are things that require our most mindful and active attention. For work, these might include the most pertinent aspects of our job descriptions—overseeing a budget, managing a long-term project that defines our business, or maintaining constant operations. For personal matters, it could mean directing our health (or that of our loved ones), sustaining a relationship or marriage, selling a house, or establishing a business. Whatever things most impact every other thing in our lives or work are the most important.

However, just because something is extremely important doesn't mean every activity that supports it needs to be done immediately. Some can be put on the backburner (indefinitely, even), some aren't even ready to be dealt with, and some depend on other people moving first. In short, you can't do them all *right now*. That's where the "urgency" metric comes in: the top row of the matrix is thus divided according to what can happen now and what can be delayed (but must happen at some point in the future).

Urgent: Do. Objects in the "do" quadrant are things that absolutely need to be done posthaste. They must be completed to stave off unfavorable outcomes or uncontrollable circumstances, and the sooner they're done, the less work (and more relief) there will be in the future. "Do" tasks typically revolve around deadlines: final term papers, court filings, car registrations, school applications, and so forth.

They also include emergencies or activities that need to be completed to avert disaster. "Do" tasks are best thought of as duties that need to be completed immediately, by the end of today, or tomorrow at the very latest. They cause anxiety because they're high-effort duties that you dread doing but need to do nevertheless.

Not urgent: Plan. Tasks that reside in the second quadrant need to be done at some point—but not necessarily *now*. The world isn't going to collapse if they're not done today; they're not on a strict deadline to be completed. Still, they have to be done at *some* point, usually relatively soon, so they need to be scheduled. "Plan" tasks include setting up a future meeting with a big client, arranging a time for a roof leak to be fixed, studying or reading class materials or work documents, or maintenance duties that cover the long term.

Schedule them after the fires are put out. Plan them for the near future, but not so imminent that it interferes with your truly urgent *and* important tasks. "Plan" tasks are also key components of your medium- to long-range plans: when you're planning a week or a month in advance, "plan" tasks should be put on your timetable.

The danger with these "not urgent" tasks is deprioritizing them too much. They're important to keep normal operations afloat, and if they're discarded or forgotten, they may well turn into emergency tasks in short order. Take the "check engine" light in your car from earlier—anecdotally, I have driven with that light on for close to a year and nothing terrible has happened, so even though it's theoretically important, it doesn't demand urgent attention.

Not-important tasks. The bottom row of Eisenhower's matrix represents tasks that aren't that significant to you personally. That doesn't mean they're unimportant to other people (though it might), but they're activities that might be more appropriate or meaningful for somebody else to finish up. Other people will certainly attempt to present them as important to you, but they're often just projecting their own self-interests. Is there an impact on you? Minimal, if any. The not-important tier is also divided up by relative urgency.

Urgent: Delegate. Perhaps the most befuddling square in this matrix is the "not-important but urgent" box. It perhaps makes the most sense in a work environment: these are tasks that might really need to be done, but it's not vital for *you* to take care of them yourself, even if you could. If you *did* complete them yourself, they might impose on the "important" items that you absolutely have to do either now or later.

For those reasons, items in this box should be eliminated, preferably by being delegated to somebody else. When you're working as the leader of a team, you should be able to find someone else to handle these tasks for you.

Not-important/urgent tasks can be identified by measuring how vital they are to what's happening now. These can very generally be described as interruptions: phone calls, emails, ongoing family situations, and so forth. During times of inactivity these all may be important to focus on, but at the moment they could distract or misdirect you from what you have to get accomplished toward your overall goals.

You may be fielding customer support emails even though you are the CEO of the 100-person company. These customer support emails represent extremely angry and disturbed clients, and they're urgent to everyone involved—except you.

There really is no point or importance for you to be involved in this daily minutia, and thus, you must eliminate it from your schedule through delegation.

Not urgent: Eliminate. Finally, there are some activities and functions that are neither important nor time-sensitive to the priorities at hand. What are they even there for? Mostly to distract you or serve as an escape from doing what you need to do: leisure activity, social media, binge-watching, long phone calls, extensive hobby time, and so forth. In the name of efficiency and prioritizing, these things are dead weight—we might not always be optimizing for those things, but it is still helpful to simply know.

These are just things that grab your attention for one reason or another and try to force a response; they're even hard to name sometimes because they feel so insignificant and fleeting. But they add up. (If you ever want to shock yourself and see how much they add up, install trackers on your phone and computer to see how much time you log on truly useless pursuits.)

These are the activities you shouldn't account for in your schedule at all and should only be done when everything else is completed. Only keep items that are important to the bottom-line success of your project or life. This doesn't mean you can't *ever* do them (and you'd be mistaken not to allow yourself a little bit of escapism now and then). But when you're in the middle of other important items that need your attention or oversight, take them off your plate completely. They'll be more meaningful and rewarding when you've finished the important tasks anyway.

Just because something appears to demand a quick response doesn't mean you should give it, and just because something is slowly ticking in the background doesn't mean you should ignore it. Learn to balance the two for optimal decisions.

Takeaways:

- Even though we know procrastination is always lurking, we can't always fight it, no matter how close attention we pay. That's why it pays to plan to avoid procrastination completely. At least you'll give yourself a much better fighting chance.
- First, you can use the STING method, by which you select one task, time yourself, ignore everything else, opt for no breaks, and give yourself a reward. It's the act of willful ignorance that makes STING so powerful. This is a scary concept, but once you resolve to only juggle one thing at a time, you'll be happy to report that

the world didn't end. You'll find that you can create STING periods, and start chaining them together with breaks between. With luck, it will become your new normal.

- Second, you can use your knowledge of the procrastination equation to your advantage by increasing both success expectancy ("I can do it") and task value ("This is worthwhile") while decreasing reward delay ("I see no immediate benefit") and impulsiveness (the *need* to engage in something). You can manipulate each of these variables to increase your motivation and momentum toward productivity. At the very least, you can recognize what factors you may be ignoring.

- Third, you can bundle temptations. This means simultaneously satisfying the hedonist in your current self and the prudence of your future self. Make both happy at the same time by pairing unpleasant tasks (future self) with sought-after pleasures (present self). You can create a win-win situation; you can also do this in the negative sense by doling out small punishments to yourself in the absence of action.

- Finally, you can use the Eisenhower matrix to distinguish between urgent and important tasks. They may overlap from time to time, but ultimately, if you are procrastinating, you are focusing too much on urgent to the detriment of important.

Chapter 6: Structuring Against Procrastination

"Tomorrow is often the busiest day of the week."
—Anonymous

Procrastination can be like a ninja who creeps up on you and hijacks your entire day without you even noticing it. How can you prevent this from happening?

One of the major strategies you can employ is to structure your day and schedule with the goal in mind of beating procrastination before it hits you. Scheduling against procrastination may not work every time, but at least it gives you a guideline to act successfully. There are a number of ways this can be done: (1) aim for no more "zero days," (2) employ self-interrogation techniques, (3) write a schedule, and (4) limit your information consumption.

Aim for No More "Zero Days"

A zero day is a day that you've let slip by without doing anything to achieve your goal. This concept may also apply to a week, an hour, or any other time segment you set (e.g., a zero year is one in which you probably hid out in a cave somewhere and hibernated for 365 days).

The concept of a zero day simplifies keeping score of how you're doing so far in working toward task completion or the achievement of your dreams. Think of life as a binary: either you're doing something ("1") or you're not ("0"). Aim for a string of 1s instead of 0s. Make it black and white with no in-between. In other words, see to it that every day you do something that'll inch you closer to your goal.

Notice the phrase "inch you closer." The idea of having no more zero days doesn't mean you have to pack every single day with tasks that'll break new ground or catapult you to immediate success. This kind of thinking is what intimidates or scares most people away from doing anything at all to accomplish their goals. They think they have to exhaust themselves with big, significant tasks every day because they believe simply pecking at something is not worth the effort.

Then, overwhelmed by the idea of having to start on a large task in front of them, they procrastinate and build a string of 0s instead. Once they accumulate two to three days of 0s, they then find it easier to let the 0s persist for the rest of the days. They may think, "*Well, I've missed three days at the gym already, so what's the point of ever going at all when I can't be consistent with this?"*

So they stop going to the gym. Others may think, *"I have to finish writing an entire chapter today. What's the point of sitting down to write if I'll add only two sentences in there?"* Then, intimidated by the thought of having to complete an entire chapter in one sitting, they simply procrastinate on the task and end up not writing a word in there at all.

So instead of seeing each day as either a 10 (task competed) or a 0 (no work done), replace the idea of needing a 10 to needing just a 1 (got something done). It doesn't matter how small of a portion of a task you managed to do for the day; it only matters that you at least got something done.

Give yourself a 1 for the day. Strive to rid your calendar of any 0 in there, but if you do slip up and get a 0 one day, don't feel discouraged. Recover the next day with another 1. Once you get into the habit of doing something every single day toward your goal, the number of 0s in your calendar will start to get fewer until it finally disappears.

For instance, say you need to write a five-chapter research paper over the course of five months. Aim to complete at least one chapter a month, and pledge to have a string of non-zeroes every month. This means that every single day, you need to get something down on paper or do something related to your research paper. Some days you may feel like an idea machine and jot down a lot of creative ways of looking at your research problem.

Other days you may feel demotivated but still read even just a single paragraph of related literature. The only thing that matters is that you incur no zero days. It might also help motivate you if you reward yourself at the end of every month that you managed to get through without ever incurring a 0.

Another example is setting a "no zero before lunch" policy for yourself. This means that you should accomplish at least a little something toward your goal before every lunch hour. The task you manage to complete may be as simple as scanning the documents needed for your database or as complex as developing a software system validation procedure. Again, the only thing that matters is that you get something done, whether big or small. It's a way to break the inertia that will cause you to find comfort in procrastinating.

Keep in mind that you can apply the "no zero" policy to a whole range of time segments, from a span of hours to years. You may choose to commit to a "no zero hour," a "no zero day," a "no zero week," and so on. The important thing is that whatever time segment you set for yourself, you see to it that you get to do something within it that'll bring you closer to completing your task.

Employ Self-Interrogation Techniques

The next time you find yourself being sweet-talked by a voice in your head saying you should just lay off a task and instead do something more enjoyable, you know what you should do? Instead of trying to drown it out by arguments (or expletives, if you're feeling especially frustrated), Peter Banerjea suggests a more creative and effective solution: ask it a question.

There are at least four questions you can keep at the ready to help you overcome procrastination the next time it tugs at you.

First, you may ask yourself, "*What one thing can I do to get started?*" Sometimes, you procrastinate mainly because you simply don't know where to start. Asking this question helps you recognize that the large task in front of you can be broken down into smaller subtasks, from which you can then select a single task to start with.

For instance, if you simply tell yourself you need to come up with an advertising plan for your product, you're more likely to procrastinate because you can't yet see the smallest possible units of action you can do to get going on that large task. To remedy this, ask yourself what the most basic, smallest possible step you can do to start is.

Maybe you realize you need to define your target market first, and the first small step toward doing that is getting a profile of your current customer base. You have thus defined a single concrete task you can direct all your energy toward, instead of floundering about, confused, until you're tempted to procrastinate. Everything huge started with a tiny step—find your tiny step and gain momentum.

Second, try to answer, *"What are my three biggest priorities today?"* As in the first question, procrastination may just be the result of not knowing what to do because of the overwhelming number of tasks before you. By asking yourself to define your main priorities, you get to narrow down your focus and address specific activities.

You get to remind yourself of what's really essential to do for the day, and in so doing, you'll be better able to spot mere distractions and evade them. Keeping your biggest priorities at the forefront of your mind ensures the spotlight is on your intended tasks and not on extraneous activities.

Suppose you're flooded by a deluge of tasks as you prepare for your company's tenth founding anniversary. Instead of fleeing the anxiety-causing scene altogether, approach it by first asking yourself to name just three main things you need to do today. For instance, you may just aim to draft the guest list, pick out a theme, and decide on a catering service before the day ends.

Third, figure out, *"How can I make this easier?"* According to habit-building expert S.J. Scott, committing to something small and easy is one of the best ways to start building a new habit. So before you take on bigger goals, see if you can first incorporate bite-sized sections of it in your schedule. Make it as easy as possible and within the flow of your day; in fact, make it difficult to *not* comply.

For example, you might find it a daunting goal to finish reading 52 books in a year. To help kick-start yourself to read, ask yourself how you can make it easier for you to incorporate reading in your daily life. You may start with a goal of reading five pages every night before you go to sleep, then gradually build up the number of pages and the times of the day you do your reading.

You might download digital versions onto your phone and place the physical version on your shoes so that you cannot avoid them. You might also make rules for no television or Internet before you read. That way, you condition yourself to get into a more manageable habit before overwhelming yourself with an entire book each time.

And fourth, ask yourself, *"What will go wrong if I don't do this now?"* Think of the worst-case scenario from time to time. Raising this question will help put things in perspective for you, especially as to how habitual procrastination can negatively impact your career and personal life. Inciting fear in yourself may not be the most positive emotional experience, but it can bring about positive results.

As you're reminded of how delaying tasks will ruin so many things for you, you'll feel more motivated to get started and keep going until you've reached your goal. By creating fear in yourself, you kick your own butt to stop bumming around and get going on things.

For instance, you might feel like procrastinating on a sales presentation you need to deliver for a potential client. To help overcome your impulse to procrastinate, consider what might go wrong if you don't get going on the task now. Really fall down the rabbit hole of potential consequences. You may leave yourself too little time to prepare adequately, which will lead you to give a horrible presentation. You might then lose that client, not to mention the confidence of your supervisor and colleagues.

This may snowball into you no longer being trusted with important tasks, spoiling your potential for professional growth and ascent on the career ladder. If you keep in mind how a single presentation can make or break the trajectory of your entire career, you'll feel a stronger motivation to stop procrastinating.

Write Down a Schedule

How do you go about a typical workday? Do you arrive at the office with a clear idea about what you need to do, the resources you'll need for it, and when you're going to do it? Or do you simply freestyle through the day, picking up whatever task catches your eye or waiting for others to usher you into one activity after another?

If you answered yes to the latter, then it's probably time for a major change. The science on productivity and efficiency at work indicates that having a schedule works better than simply winging it. In a study published by the *British Journal of Health Psychology*, just under 250 adults were assessed as to their motivation to exercise.

They were divided into three groups, all instructed to keep track of how often they exercised over the course of two weeks, but each was given different conditions: (1) the control group was asked to read a few lines of a neutral book; (2) Group A (motivation) was given a pamphlet outlining how exercise can decrease the risk of heart disease; and (3) Group B (intention) was treated the same way as Group A, with the additional instruction to set a detailed exercise schedule over the course of two weeks. Group B identified when they would exercise, how long each workout would be, and where their workouts would take place.

The outcome? While only 35% of Group A ended up working out once a week, 91% of Group B (those who scheduled their exercise) were able to accomplish the said routine. This goes to show how scheduling can dramatically improve your likelihood of following through on tasks with respect to a goal. So if scheduling is so helpful, how do you do it?

Scheduling involves identifying a number of elements. First, identify the tasks that you need to do. Second, decide when you're going to do each task. Assign a specific time frame (e.g., "from 8:30 a.m. to 9:30 a.m.") instead of using vague terms (e.g., "sometime in the morning").

Third, identify the tools and resources you'll need for the task so that you can prepare them beforehand. Fourth, name the physical location where you'll carry out each task. This way, you'll know exactly where to head to when the scheduled time arrives. Finally, draft a backup plan in case the task doesn't get done in the scheduled slot. Write down all of these details on a piece of paper, then post it someplace you can always see it as a reminder of how your day is supposed to go.

Scheduling helps you start your day knowing what you need to do and when you're going to do it so you don't even have to spend as much energy and willpower racking your brain throughout the day, agonizing over which important task you need to complete next. With a schedule, you get to simply follow a clear time-and-motion guide: for a particular time frame, there's a particular action you're directed to do. This will allow you to smoothly and efficiently go from one task to another throughout the day.

Again, the absence of downtime for constructive thought ends up helping you here.

Scheduling also allows you to visualize things such that you can see pockets of time within the day in which you can insert certain activities. For example, you've identified that you have a morning meeting from 10:00 a.m. to 11:00 a.m. Based on that, you see that your 8:00 a.m. to 10:00 a.m. slot is actually free and is time you could use to accomplish tasks rather than just waiting for the meeting to start. So to maximize your morning, schedule a task that you estimate will take about two hours to complete for that time slot.

By scheduling, you also get to appreciate just how much time you can afford to spend on a task. You'll be prevented from procrastinating when you see there's a danger of the completion of one task eating away at a time frame you've set for another activity.

You can actually go a step beyond mere scheduling and make a commitment to living in your calendar. There are 168 hours in any given week, and once you fill in your calendar, you'll know exactly what you should be doing at each moment. It just might force you to work a bit quicker and more efficiently and tune out your distractions in pursuit of staying on track in your calendar.

Limit Information Consumption

It happens all the time. You're sitting down, trying to get in some reading, and by the time you look up, hours have passed. Losing track of time in this pursuit is great if you're being productive, but reading is only productive when it adds actual value to our lives. More often than not, it doesn't!

Consuming information is almost always seen as a net positive. It's what we think underlies being educated and intelligent, and reading in particular is seen as superior to more passive forms of media consumption.

The point is that it's easy to feel like we're being productive by reading, when all we're actually doing is wasting time in a slightly more intellectual way than binge-watching *Game of Thrones*. When we justify our information consumption in this way, what we're really doing is justifying our procrastination. We use information as a procrastination tool. Reclaim your lost time and get started by going on an *information diet*.

Information diets aren't about being less educated or cutting out leisure reading; it's just about considering what our end goals are and if we are unconsciously doing something detrimental to those goals. Too often and too easily, we get *sucked into* information, so it must be limited to keep your working mood.

But how do we decide what information is worth consuming, and what's worth leaving on the shelf? How do we even know what information is sucking up our time? Begin by taking an honest look at how you spend your time. You can do this in the following steps.

1. Survey your information consumption.
2. Remove at least 50% of the least valuable information you consume and cut the noise from your information diet.
3. View descriptions of information pieces as pitches for your time and attention.
4. Say no more often.
5. Consider cutting entire information forms from your life.
6. Monitor how much of any one information source you're consuming.

For one week, make a list of every type of media you consume, from your Facebook feed to *War and Peace*.

It's important to know exactly where your time is going so you can make cuts. You might be surprised to find you're scrolling through social media feeds for hours per day, or you may find that you spend far too many hours consuming the latest bestseller. It doesn't matter what you're consuming when you begin this process; what matters is that you identify where your time is going so that you can redirect it toward activities that need to get done.

After you make your list, you'll see a lot of different mediums. Social media, books, magazines, television, podcasts, and similar items will probably populate your list. Some are genuinely valuable; they help you be more creative, bring you joy, and make you and your life better. They assist you in your work, or they are flat-out required research to keep you progressing and growing. This doesn't all have to be edifying; genuinely enjoying a TV show or other product can be a good enough reason to keep it in your life.

But right off the bat, you can also see that some of these are useless and just keep you stuck in inaction. You'll find a lot of items that you didn't actively choose to watch or read; they were just there, in front of you, and you consumed them on autopilot. Autopilot as unconscious consumption is the real enemy here.

You can tell something should be cut out of your life when it has no current or practical utility. Only information we can immediately apply to our current situation is important. This is what happens when we fall into the Wikipedia rabbit hole, for instance—suddenly we end up learning about 17th-century woodworking when we were only trying to learn about one historical figure.

Hypothetical or "just in case" information can also be useful, but most of the time it shouldn't be your current focus. This is like researching the type of clothing you should buy when you lose 50 pounds—it's a legitimate concern, but not at the present moment.

Plenty of other information you consume will be downright useless—you neither enjoy it nor find facts within it that can be applied to better your life. It was just placed in front of you, and you consumed it without realizing it. These are cereal boxes, advertisements, and vapid entertainment news that are just entertaining enough to suck us in but are mostly without substance.

Once you cut out 50% of the least useful media you consume, you'll have that much more spare time to devote to the things you've been putting off. That's way better than wasting time skimming through posts or blankly watching a show you don't care about. This in itself isn't a cure for procrastination, but it does help when you are at the fork in the road, and if a distraction is less handy, it's one less obstacle to working.

It helps to view television, books, articles, and podcasts as pitches for your time and attention. Both are finite; everything we consume also consumes our time and energy. In addition, we can't produce at the same time as we're consuming. It's impossible to do both at once.

At this point, it should be obvious that being entertained or even being educated doesn't come free of cost, even when no money is being charged. Even when items are free, they're not without cost to your work and productivity.

Given all of this, it makes sense to be discriminating about what we spend our time consuming and to be especially careful before we let something new catch our eye. Before watching or reading anything, even something you know you'll like, read or listen to a short description and consider whether the object is worth your time. You can even do this with works you already know by consciously reminding yourself what you're going to find before loading up a website or sitting down for a film. The important thing here is consciousness. When we think about the cost of frittering away time on subpar entertainment, we're less likely to indulge—or to waste time.

In addition to considering the inherent cost of consuming information, there's a much simpler way to change our habits: commit to saying no. Merely deciding to stop ourselves from indulging in media a set number of times, say three times per week, can radically change how we interact with the world.

Without consciously setting limits, it's easy to see keeping up with friends on social media as an obligation or to feel like we have to finish watching the show we like, but none of that's compulsory. At all points, we control our action. We can always say no.

While filtering things out of your life and preventing your newfound autonomy from being snatched from you, consider the mediums that deliver low-value information to you. Often, we find ourselves drifting back to the same time sinks over and over again. When we notice these patterns, it's worth considering excising the whole medium from our lives. Whether it's getting rid of cable TV, committing to a life without social media, or deciding to spend less time reading books, making a decisive change can prevent the need to say no over and over again.

The relaxation inherent in not having to think about checking a source of media in the modern age is phenomenal. It not only frees you to spend time creating or to spend time with the people you love, but it also lifts pressure from our shoulders. And if you selected the medium to ax well, that's doubly true.

Finally, consider how much time you're sinking into all the remaining forms of media you consume. How much time is spent on television, reading, listening to podcasts, or scrolling through feeds?

If you spend too much time in any one place, it's likely you're spending time on those activities because they're an automatic thing for you to do, not because you're really enjoying them. Cutting back in those areas can leave more time for the good things in life.

Learning to make cutbacks on attention expenditures lets us focus on information that helps us grow, learn, and thrive. Fortunately, the process of reducing the noise from your media streams can be approached in many ways, allowing anyone to make small—or even major—changes in their routines.

Once we've established a newer, more conscious routine, it'll be that much easier to find time for the people and things we truly love and to finish tasks we'd otherwise be inclined to set aside. That sure beats being constantly stressed about the work we're avoiding.

Takeaways:

- This chapter is about how to structure your day to prevent procrastination. Will it work every time, every day? No, but you stand a much better chance when you engage in these exercises than when you don't. Procrastination leaps on you when you have idle time and when you're unengaged. Scheduling and structuring prevents this and attempts to take the decision out of your hands entirely.
- The first step in scheduling is more about how to approach your schedule and day structure. Namely, pledge to yourself to have no more "zero days," where a zero day is a day that you've let slip by without doing anything to achieve your goal. You can also substitute an hour, week, or a minute in place of a day. In any case, having the

intention to just act in every time segment will help prevent procrastination.

- Self-interrogation questions can also help you when you're on the cusp of procrastinating. If you ask yourself a certain set of questions, you are able to immediately take a step and break through the inertia. The questions are as follows: What is one thing I can do right now? What are my top three priorities today? How can I make this easier for me to follow through? And what will go wrong if I don't try to persevere?

- Truly scheduling everything into your agenda works because it lets you visually understand what needs to be done. This effect can be further enhanced if you schedule, along with the task itself, where you will perform it, what resources are needed, and when it should be done. The more details and specificity, the better. You can take this a step further by living in your calendar and accounting for all of your 168 hours a week.

- Finally, you can limit your information consumption. Very little of what we consume is helpful or even relevant. Most of it is also consumed unconsciously, without us realizing that we are spending so much time and effort on it—we get sucked in. Cultivate self-awareness and curate your consumption and reduce your media sources so you can devote your limited energy toward work and motion.

Chapter 7. Get Off Your Butt

"The only difference between success and failure is the ability to take action."
—Alexander Graham Bell

In this chapter, I wanted to cover one of procrastination's biggest enemies: the immediate moment. Of course, we know procrastination is the devil on our shoulders that suggests we will be totally fine if we push what we should do until another moment, then another, then another, and then a few more after the next four. You get the idea.

What is it that makes us want to say "I'll get to it later!" in the hopes that it will disappear forever? Whatever it is, this chapter is aimed at just getting started as a way to break inertia.

The 40-70 Rule

Can you actually be too prepared? Is this causing you to procrastinate?

Former U.S. Secretary of State Colin Powell has a rule of thumb about coming to a point of action. He says that any time you face a hard choice, you should have *no less* than 40% and *no more* than 70% of the information you need to make that decision. In that range, you have enough information to make an informed choice, but not so much intelligence that you lose your resolve and simply stay abreast of the situation.

If you have less than 40% of the information you need, you're essentially shooting from the hip. You don't know quite enough to move forward and will probably make a lot of mistakes. Conversely, if you chase down more data until you get more than 70% of what you need (and it's unlikely that you'll truly need anything above this level), you could get overwhelmed and uncertain. The opportunity may have passed you by, and someone else may have beaten you by starting already.

This is the zone of procrastination—you want 100% information, and although it's never possible, it's a zone of safety.

But in that sweet spot between 40% and 70%, you have enough to go on and let your intuition guide your decisions. In the context of Colin Powell, this is where effective leaders are made: the people who have instincts that point in the right direction are who will lead their organizations to success. This is also where you should battle procrastination before it becomes too late. You should feel a certain amount of uncertainty or even lack of confidence—it's natural, and anything else is an unrealistic expectation. More often than not, what you are searching for will only be gained through *beginning*.

We can replace the word "information" with other motivators: 40–70% of experience, 40–70% reading or learning, 40–70%

confidence, or 40–70% of planning. While we're taking action, we learn, gain confidence, and gain momentum.

When you try to achieve more than 70% information (or confidence, experience, etc.), your lack of speed can destroy your momentum or stem your interest, effectively meaning nothing's going to happen. There is a high likelihood of gaining nothing further from surpassing this threshold.

For example, let's say you're opening up a cocktail bar, which involves buying a lot of different types of liquor. You're going to wait until you're 100% ready with your liquor before opening.

You can't expect to have absolutely all the liquor you will ever need when the doors are ready to open. It's impossible to be able to serve any drink that a customer orders.

So, applying this rule, you'd wait until you had at least 40% of your available inventory prepared. This would establish momentum. Then, if you could get more than half of what you need, you'd be in pretty good shape to open. You might not be able to make absolutely every drink in the bartender's guide, but you'll have enough on hand to cover the staple drinks with a couple of variations. If you have around 50–60% inventory, you're more than ready. When the remaining inventory arrives, you'll already be in action and can just incorporate that new inventory into your offerings. If you waited until you had 70% or more inventory, you could find yourself stuck in neutral for longer than you wanted to be.

This way of thinking leads to more action than not. Waiting until you have 40% of what you need to make a move isn't a way of staying inside your comfort zone—you're actively planning what you need to do to get out, which is just fine (as long as it's not over-planning).

Tiny Steps

Very few people want to go to work when it's raining cats and dogs outside.

It's an enormous burden to overcome mentally. You'll get soaked, your shoes and socks will be puddles, and you'll freeze from head to toe. Oh, and your only umbrella is broken. It's such a burden that you don't even want to go through the motions of getting dressed and putting on your boots. You feel defeated before you even get started.

Sometimes a horrendously rainy day can feel just like trying to be productive.

When we're faced with huge tasks that feel insurmountable, it's like looking through a window out at the rain. It's such an obstacle that everything feels impossible and pointless. We drag our feet, discourage ourselves, and bitterly complain the whole time.

But that's the wrong way to look at the tasks on our plates.

A single huge task, such as "finish the 200-page report," can certainly sound imposing, if not impossible. However, what if you were to break that monumental task up into tiny, individual, easy tasks you could get to work on immediately? For example: preparing the template, finding the first three sources, creating a bibliography, outlining 500 words of the first section, and so on. Actually, it can go much smaller yet: choosing the fonts, writing the chapter titles, organizing the desk, formatting the document, or writing just one sentence. The smaller, the better; otherwise, you're starting each day staring at the equivalent of a rainy day. Your end is to start with tasks that barely feel like you're doing anything at all.

One of the biggest hurdles to productivity is looking at tasks as huge, inseparable boulders. It's intimidating and discouraging, and when those emotions arise, it's tough to avoid procrastinating because tackling a boulder is a tough sell. Unfortunately, this is a habit that plagues most people. They see only massive boulders and allow themselves to get emotionally thrown off track.

Break up your big tasks into smaller tasks, and keep repeating until the tasks you have before you are so easy you can do them within a few minutes. Create small, manageable chunks that will be psychologically uplifting and acceptable, and you'll kick your production up instantly. Make your to-do list as long and articulated as possible, with as many small tasks as you can list. A pebble is something you can do instantly, without any effort, and even with little thought.

Productivity is nothing without action, and action is much easier with something simple and easy to warm up with. Small steps can take you to the top of the hill and let you roll down the other side to seize momentum. They help you break the inertia that leads you to passivity and inaction.

Let's take an example that we're all familiar with: working out. You want to lose 100 pounds, a hefty goal.

If you go into the gym every day thinking that you want to lose 100 pounds, you're probably going to fail. It's a huge, enormous boulder of a goal. It might sound grand to proclaim, but in reality, it is going to be very hard to stick to because of how unbelievable it sounds.

You won't see much progress on a daily or even weekly basis, and you will understandably become discouraged. It's too much to face at once, like the rainy day from the beginning of the chapter. What if you approached your weight loss goal by breaking it into small, manageable increments (goals) and tasks?

This might look something like setting a reasonable weekly weight loss goal, creating daily goals of eating specific foods (and not eating others) and drinking water every hour. Eat 100 fewer calories per meal. Go on walks after each meal. Drink only half your soda. Eat five fewer fries each meal. Cook once a week. Buy the low-calorie version of snacks.

If you hit your weekly weight loss goal and successfully drink water every hour, it is far easier to stay motivated and focused. Meeting your smaller, weekly goal will give you a sense of accomplishment, whereas making an insignificant dent in your total goal (100 pounds) will only make you feel discouraged and as if the task ahead is too great to achieve.

These are small tasks that, if done consistently and correctly, will lead to your overall goal of losing 100 pounds.

These small victories will encourage and motivate you—and so it is with tasks, productivity, and procrastination. Don't underestimate the power of small victories.

Banish Excuses

People use excuses to postpone taking action and to procrastinate. Most excuses, however, are poppycock—invalid, rubbish, and rationalized. Excuses are our subconscious protecting us from our fears. It is your automatic pilot saying, "Danger! This might not go well! Let me save you!" Let's look at some common excuses people use to procrastinate.

Now is not the right time. Related variations: *I can't do X until... I can't do X unless...* True. There is never a perfect time for anything. There are mediocre times and terrible times, but rarely are there perfect times. Stop putting conditions around your ability to work. All you are doing is creating a psychological gatekeeper for yourself that is detrimental.

Timing is everything—that's actually not true. Timing just *is*. There is no good time for a crisis, but they happen anyway. When trying to be productive, rarely is there an obvious time that is better than another. It's just a lie we tell ourselves. There are always going to be obstacles to overcome and hassles to manage. In fact, 99% of the time you want to do something, the timing will be mediocre, 1% of the timing will be truly terrible, and that's it. There should never be any expectations of having perfect timing.

When is the right time to travel? When is the right time to get married? When is the right time to have a child? When is the right time to quit? You know the answer to these questions.

For instance, there is never a perfect time to sell a house. The housing market is unpredictable, and various rates are subject to change overnight. You also don't know what bids you will receive and if anyone will even view your home. On the other hand, there are some objectively horrible times to sell a house, like when a main employer in town lays off 50% of its workforce and interest rates take a 10% rise.

Many of us wish timing was something we had more control over, but the fact remains that we rarely get to choose when something happens to us. We do, however, get to choose when we take action. If you find yourself questioning this, the time to act has already arrived.

I don't know where to start. You do; the problem is that you think you need an entire plan before starting. People need to stop expecting to see a clear path through to the end before they even begin.

Here is the secret: you don't need to know where you'll will finish in order to start. The number one college major for students entering university in the U.S. is *undecided*. Most 18-year-olds are not able to articulate what they want to study that will lead to a lifelong career. However, we encourage young people to get to college soon after high school. "Don't wait too long. Don't get too many responsibilities." During the four (or five) years they are on campus, most students declare a major and start working toward a degree that will eventually lead to employment.

We think nothing of this process; however, so many times in adulthood people become paralyzed because they don't see a clear finish line. Doing something today with what you have today is the key. Stop researching, stop agonizing, stop wasting time, and start doing. Do what you can do right now at this very moment, and you can figure out the next steps after. You probably know your next steps, however small they may be.

The blank page or the blank screen is the writer's nightmare. It does not matter if the writer is a middle schooler with a book report due or Stephen King. The blank page is terrifying. And yet, all who eventually produced something to fill that paper or screen had to stop reading the book, stop researching the topic, stop planning out the flow, and just start writing.

The first words written may not be any good. They may be terrible and need to be changed. But the writer cannot get there if they never write any words down. The way to start writing is simple: start writing. Focusing on the end product, a hardback with a glossy cover, isn't the goal at the beginning. A beginning is the goal. After you start, the rest will take care of itself because you will know what needs to be done to get you to the next step and then the one after that.

I'm not good enough. Shockingly, that just might be true. A person may really want to do something, but they might not be good enough. What is the answer to that dilemma? You can *become* good enough.

Sometimes the only way to get what you want is to shift into a growth mindset and start working. Make sure that this time next year, you know more than you know now and that your skills are better than they are now. If you are willing to take the first steps, what you need will follow.

When you feel like you are not good enough, you might need to reframe it just a bit to "I'm not good enough at this moment." After all, why would anyone have the expectation that they would be good enough at something without practice, work, and a significant amount of time? You simply cannot have the expectation of instant or even preemptive excellence. If you never start, you will never be good enough, and you will have prophesized your own future.

Learning a musical instrument is an illustrative example. When people say they aren't musical before picking up an instrument, it makes little sense, doesn't it? If learning to play the piano is your goal, then you can certainly make it happen. You would have to start back at that beginning middle C, but with lessons, practice, patience, and perseverance.

Anyone, including you, can learn to play the piano. Who knows? Perhaps you could eventually become a keyboard player for a Queen cover band. Just because you are not good enough now does not mean you cannot become good enough eventually.

Combating excuses is difficult because of our overwhelming need for self-protection. We may not even realize when we are using defense mechanisms to procrastinate, but chances are if you find yourself justifying a lack of action, it's a defense mechanism.

Parkinson's Law

Parkinson's Law states that *work expands so as to fill the time available for its completion*. Whatever deadline you give yourself, big or small, that's how long you'll take to complete the work. If you give yourself a relaxed deadline, you avoid being disciplined; if you give yourself a tight deadline, you can draw on your self-discipline.

Bureaucrat Cyril Parkinson observed that as bureaucracies expanded, their efficiency decreased instead of increased. The more space and time people were given, the more they took—something that he realized was applicable to a wide range of other circumstances. The general form of the law became that increasing the size of something decreases its efficiency.

As it relates to focus and time, Parkinson found that simple tasks would be made increasingly more complex in order to fill the time allotted to their completion. Decreasing the available time for completing a task caused that task to become simpler and easier and completed in a timelier fashion.

Building on Parkinson's Law, a study of college students found that those who imposed strict deadlines on themselves for completing assignments consistently performed better than those who gave themselves an excessive amount of time and those who set no limits at all. Why?

The artificial limitations they had set for their work caused them to be far more efficient than their counterparts. They didn't spend a lot of time worrying about the assignments because they didn't give themselves the time to indulge. They got to work, finished the projects, and moved on. They also didn't have time to ruminate on what ultimately didn't matter—a very common type of subtle procrastination. They were able to subconsciously focus on only the elements that mattered to completing the assignment.

Very few people are ever going to require you or even ask you to work less. So if you want to be more productive and efficient, you'll have to avoid falling victim to Parkinson's Law by applying artificial limitations on the time you give yourself to complete tasks. By simply giving yourself time limits and deadlines for your work, you force yourself to focus on the crucial elements of the task. You don't make things more complex or difficult than they need to be just to fill the time.

For example, say that your supervisor gives you a spreadsheet and asks you to make a few charts from it by the end of the week. The task might take an hour, but after looking over the spreadsheet you notice that it's disorganized and difficult to read, so you start editing it. This takes an entire week, but the charts you were supposed to generate would only have taken an hour. If you had been given the deadline of one day, you would have simply focused on the charts and ignored everything that wasn't important. When we are given the space, as Parkinson's Law dictates, we expand our work to fill the time.

Set aggressive deadlines so that you are actually challenging yourself on a consistent basis, and you'll avoid this pitfall. A distant deadline also typically means a sustained level of background stress—push yourself to finish early and free your mind. Save your time by giving yourself less time.

The Energy Pyramid

When we put off our work, it's often because we have too little energy to do what needs to be done. When we experience our work as draining, we're too tired to focus, we're easily distracted, and we feel like we can't accomplish the job we've been assigned, what we're really experiencing are symptoms of poor energy management.

This is a bigger problem than we realize, because even more so than time, energy is a finite resource that we must protect on a daily basis. Nothing else you read in this book will make an iota of difference if you don't have the energy to pull it off.

Energy drains, and once it does, recharging is necessary. One great tool to understand energy management is the energy pyramid, an idea conceived by Jim Loehr and Tony Schwartz in *The Power of Full Engagement:*

Managing Energy, Not Time, is the Key to High Performance and Personal Renewal.

The energy pyramid is a four-tiered pyramid with *physical energy* at its base, *emotional energy* above that, *mental energy* in the next layer, and *spiritual energy* at the top. Each of these plays an important role in building up or draining our energy, and each tier depends upon the tiers below to sustain itself. Understanding the interconnected nature of what goes into the energy we have for work allows us to take charge and create more for ourselves. Put another way, if you don't satisfy these levels of energy and engagement, it's unlikely that you will even be in a position to be able to focus and work, much less conquer procrastination.

To manage our energy, the pyramid points out that we must first notice and improve our levels of physical energy. Physical energy forms the basis for all the other tiers; it's the foundation upon which all our energy needs are built. To manage our physical energy, we mind our physical health. We eat healthy, get enough sleep, and exercise.

That may sound draining, and sometimes it is. After all, if you're not used to eating vegetables, indigestion will be the initial response to your newly healthy diet. But with time and persistence, eating well pays off with adjusted gut flora and an excess of energy. Exercise works the same way. At first, exercising feels draining, and we finish our routines exhausted. But after we've done it for a week or two, we start to feel energized when we've finished. What used to be difficult becomes easy, and when it does, it comes with a burst of fresh energy to apply to the rest of our lives.

Sleep, at least, is an activity that always feels good when we're doing it. While plenty of us wish we didn't need to sleep and could keep working without respite, it's a nonnegotiable fact of life that humans need rest. Without sleep, we yawn, have trouble focusing, and eventually fall asleep amidst our required activities. By contrast, when we put effort into getting our sleep, we're energized, ready for our day, able to focus, and unlikely to fall into an ill-timed slumber.

The best part about the physical foundation of the energy pyramid is that it's not an absolute scale. We don't have to become as athletic as teenagers, as health conscious as dieticians, or as well rested as Winnie the Pooh to benefit from healthy changes. All we have to do is find room for improvement, then improve. The benefits are almost immediate, and noticing and focusing on how much better minding our health makes us feel can motivate us to continue improving.

Once we start improving our physical health, we'll have the energy to consider the next level of the pyramid, emotional energy. Tending to our physical needs first is essential because our emotions depend upon our physical health. When we're too tired or hungry or malnourished to think clearly, we simply can't focus on emotional pursuits.

Emotions that don't result directly from our physiological state can help or hinder our ability to work, as well. Positive emotions like joy, anticipation, excitement, or even feeling challenged increase our engagement and our energy. By contrast, negative emotions like anxiety, frustration, sadness, anger, and bitterness crush us like heavy weights.

When we're overcome by these emotions, it's difficult to focus on our work and apply ourselves. But emotions aren't things we choose. Sometimes we're anxious when we know we'll be fine, and sometimes we're angry when we know we have no right to feel mad. Sometimes terrible things happen, and we feel sad or wronged; but even when negative emotions are justified, they don't help us learn, grow, and add value to the world.

The best weapon against these modern monsters is *reframing*. When you face a challenge you don't think you can overcome, don't lament the inevitably of failure, but think about how much you can learn and grow even if you lose—after all, it's exactly those sorts of failures that form the foundation of success. No one accomplishes everything on the first attempt; failure is what teaches us what to do differently to perform better in the future. A sense of being wronged and a base desire for revenge against the universe is one of the more common negative emotions that can be easily overcome by a shift in focus. The majority of what's happening in anyone's life is never bad.

Feeling good is essential to doing good. Focusing on those tiny gifts and cultivating gratitude goes a long way toward making us emotionally healthy. To feel good, we have to be willing to let go of negative emotions and be grateful for the positive aspects of all things. Happiness flows freely when we do our part, and when we're happy, we're both more energetic and better at finishing our tasks.

Mental energy is the third tier of the energy pyramid. For us to be mentally energetic, we must first be emotionally and physically energized, otherwise our exhaustion or unhappiness will be too difficult to overcome. Mental energy relates to everthing about our conscious thoughts and it allows us to be productive.

This tier asks us to take control of our thoughts. Instead of passively accepting the first thought that comes to mind, we can assess our thoughts and respond to them in order to consciously choose what we think. This will modify our outlook, allowing us to determine whether we're expecting the worst or anticipating great things.

When we make the right choices, our work is easier to handle; we can even be energized by a problem we encounter because it will feel more like a puzzle than a harbinger of our own destruction.

An important part of building mental energy is to go into tasks with optimism. When we go into things with a negative outlook, we presume we will fail. For example, children often won't try new foods because they "don't look" tasty. Often, if we can convince kids to try food despite their initial judgment, they won't like the taste, either. They'd already made up their mind that the food wasn't good, which is the reason they disliked it. But the opposite is also true; when kids look at food and think they might like it or when they're convinced to withhold judgment, they often enjoy new foods.

It's the same with adults and tasks we need to complete. When we go in excited to show what we can do, we often do a superb job; if we go in presuming we'll fail, it's often hard to produce any work at all. On top of that, we're drumming up fear from the previous tier while we tell ourselves it's not going to work.

Aside from optimism, several tools can get us in the right mental mindset. Self-talk, where we engage in dialogue with ourselves, can dismiss less helpful thoughts and give us truer narratives to believe. Internal pep talks can work, too.

Visualizing the completed project can give a sense of reality to the finished process, and meditation uses our minds to calm the tension we can retain physically and emotionally. Even managing our time better can come into play at this level of the energy pyramid, as our minds are what we use to schedule our time and assess how long tasks could and should take.

When we manage our time, guide our emotions, and make sure our thoughts are helping instead of hindering us, we'll have more energy and find it easier to face the tasks before us.

After our minds are managed, we face the peak of the pyramid, spiritual energy. This isn't a religious or spiritual tier; rather, it encourages us to understand our core values and to align our actions with those values. For example, a person who values helping people might do excellently in healthcare jobs but flounder horribly in sales jobs because their values are met in one career path but not in the other.

The spiritual tier is about finding purpose in our work, which is the best motivator that exists. Personal drive only happens when our actions are aligned with our core values. To do that, we must choose work that aligns with our values and get away from work that runs counter to what we consider important in life.

When we're doing what we feel is important, there is strong motivation to keep going and to be glad when we accomplish tasks. Aligning ourselves with our work is the strongest motivator that exists.

Physical, emotional, mental, and spiritual energy are all part of the first principle of energy management. When we attain everything the pyramid implies, we're certain to be bursting with energy, but we won't yet know how to direct and manage that energy effectively. In fact, we may be so enthusiastic about what we're doing that we risk burnout.

How do we avoid that? With the second principle: every time we use energy, we must also allow for its renewal. No one, no matter how much energy they have, can keep going at full bore forever. Rest is necessary, not just for our physical bodies, but also for our minds and hearts.

When we don't take a break from what we do, we eventually become stressed out and frustrated; these are negative emotions that are often accompanied by negative thoughts. Both will sap energy quickly.

To prevent this, we must disengage regularly so that our minds can heal. Overuse, even overuse of energy, leads to destruction of the resource that's being overused. Rest is what allows us to heal and grow stronger.

Contrasting with the second principle, the third principle of energy management reminds us that pushing past our limits is necessary for growth. We can't just sit idly, work consistently, and expect to improve. We must regularly challenge ourselves if we want to grow.

Dancers know this very well. Everyone shows up to their first class barely able to point their toes and unable to point their toes to the degree the teacher desires. But pushing allows muscles to grow stronger and the body to take new forms. Sometimes it takes years of persistent effort to reach our true goals, but the way to get there is always by setting up a challenge and getting closer and closer as our bodies, emotions, minds, and spirits allow.

Even nonphysical tasks require us to push ourselves into discomfort, as anyone who's done a bit of public speaking will know.

Most are terrified the first few times, and often that terror is discernible to the audience. Speakers will shake, stutter, and go over sections of their speech multiple times. At first, it feels like it will never get better, but persistence makes the nervous speaker reassume their task despite the difficulty. Slowly, giving speeches becomes easier. Eventually, the truly persistent will discover that it's an enjoyable activity. But none of that is possible without feeling spurred on to succeed by the challenge of public speaking. At every level, we benefit from challenging ourselves and pushing ourselves into new and difficult circumstances.

The fourth, and final, principle of energy management states that we must create energy rituals to sustain full engagement. Despite the human ability to think and choose, most of our actions are based on habit. What we do, we usually don't think about. What we have to think about, we usually don't do, at least not for very long! That means that it's essential to transform energy-sustaining practices into persistent habits so that we don't have to remember or talk ourselves into helpful habits.

This will come as no surprise to anyone who's dieted in their life; generally speaking, any short-term starvation will lead to eating in our habitual way once we shed the weight. What happens next? The weight comes back, and we have to diet again. This is particularly damaging, as each time we fail to make a real and lasting change in our life, the return of the old actions and their consequences feels more and more inevitable. It's not inevitable, but avoiding the trap involves making real, permanent changes. The new way has to be sustainable; in short, it has to become a habit.

Two months of consistently performing any action will generally turn it into a habit, but until we reach that point, we have to put active effort into creating a new routine. We must make a choice not to eat certain foods, to go and exercise, or to drink a certain amount of water. But commitment and consistency is only needed at first. Eventually, thinking becomes unnecessary; we will have the rituals in place to be healthy, happy, and effective at our work.

Once we have the habits in place to maximize our productivity, and once we become used to challenging ourselves and resting to recharge our batteries, it becomes easier to direct our energy in any way we need. When we have enough energy, even the tasks we like to avoid become easy to face!

Takeaways:

- Getting off your butt might be the very essence of conquering procrastination. Procrastination's mortal enemy is the immediate, present moment. So how do we seize that?
- Utilize the 40–70 rule as popularized by Colin Powell. This rule states the following: you only need between 40% and 70% of the information, confidence,

time, or preparation that you think you do. Anything else is just spinning your wheels and procrastinating, and 100% of what you want is impossible from the starting line. So take action at 70%, at worst, because things won't improve by simply waiting longer.

- Tiny steps are the best steps. Large tasks look intimidating and impossible. But when you break each boulder down into small pebbles that can be taken care of instantaneously and effortlessly, then you have a chance to build momentum and take care of what needs to be done in short order.

- We are full of excuses for the protection of our ego. But of course, excuses are detrimental to your working spirit. It's important to realize that these excuses are largely fabrications. "Not right now"—there is never a perfect time. "I'm not good enough"—no, but you can become good enough. "I don't know where to start"—start with what you can do right now, not only with an ultimate endpoint in mind.

- Pay attention to the energy pyramid. Energy, more than time and more than anything else, is what determines how much we get done. It is the scarcest resource because it drains on a daily basis. There are four aspects/levels to it, and each contributes to overall being able to focus and work: physical (no fatigue), emotional (no unhappiness), mental (no discouragement), and spiritual (no lack of purpose).

Summary Guide

Before getting to the overall book summary… I would be highly, greatly, amazingly grateful and appreciative if you felt like taking just 30 seconds and leaving me a review on Amazon! Reviews are incredibly important to an author's livelihood, and they are shockingly hard to come by. Strange, right?

Anyway, the more reviews my books get, the more I am actually able to continue my first love of writing. If you felt any way about this book, please leave me a review and let me know that I'm on the right track. CLICK HERE TO REVIEW

Chapter 1. Why You're a Couch Potato

- Procrastination has been around far longer than you or me. The term "procrastination" was derived from the

Latin *pro*, meaning "forward, forth, or in favor of" and *crastinus*, meaning "of tomorrow." In everyday terms, it's when you put off something unpleasant, usually in pursuit of something more pleasurable or enjoyable. In this first chapter, we discuss the typical causes of procrastination.

- This begins with the cycle of procrastination, which has five stages: unhelpful/false assumptions, increasing discomfort, excuse-making, avoidance activities, and consequences. Focus on dispelling your false assumptions, dissecting your excuses, and understanding your avoidance activities.
- The pleasure principle is important to understand in the context of procrastination. Our brains have a constant civil war brewing inside; the impulsive and largely subconscious lizard brain wants immediate pleasure at the expense of the slower prefrontal cortex, which makes rational decisions. The prefrontal cortex makes the unpopular decisions that

procrastination is not a fan of, while the lizard brain makes decisions that lead to dopamine and adrenaline being produced. It may seem like a losing battle, but the key to battling procrastination is being able to regulate our impulses and drives—though not suppress them.

- You might simply be an impulsive person. Four traits make up impulsivity: urgency (I must do this right now), lack of premeditation (I don't know how this will affect me later), lack of perseverance (I'm tired of this; what else is there to do?), and sensation-seeking (oh, that feels better than what I am currently doing). The more elevated your levels, the more impulsive and procrastinating you will be.

- A helpful method for defeating procrastination is called HALT, and it stands for hunger, anger, loneliness, or tiredness. When you are facing a fork in the road in regards to persevering or procrastinating, ask yourself if any of the

HALT factors are present. If any are, understand that you are already predisposed to making a poor decision and try to regulate your thoughts.

- It's been found that there are nine specific traits associated with procrastination: (1) inhibition, (2) self-monitoring, (3) planning and organization, (4) activity shifting, (5) task initiation, (6) task monitoring, (7) emotional control, (8) working memory, and (9) general orderliness. Generally, deficiencies in any of these nine traits will make an individual more susceptible to procrastination. To beat procrastination, we must perform one of the hardest tasks of all: thinking about one's own thinking.

Chapter 2. Your Procrastination Profile

- This chapter is about the warning signs that procrastination is imminent. There are far too many to name, but there are a few common types that can be helpful to articulate and then diagnose in yourself.

They come in the context that there are generally five different types of procrastinators: (1) thrill-seeker, (2) avoider, (3) indecisive, (4) perfectionist, and (5) busy. Each type has its own triggers, like the feeling of adrenaline and risk, avoiding rejection, and feeling overwhelmed. They can generally be grouped into two general kinds of procrastination triggers: action-based and mental/emotion-based. These speak to the physical environment and to lack of confidence and security, respectively.

- Finally, procrastination has been shown to be useful from time to time, even though it can lead to our downfall. It can improve your efficiency, clear out the rest of our to-do list, and protect yourself from hasty decisions and failure.

Chapter 3: Action Mindsets

- Procrastination may be a reflection of battling biological forces, and we can swing the battle in our favor if we use some of the mindset tactics in this chapter. Fear is an understated underlying cause of procrastination.

- The first such tactic is to understand how Newton's three laws of motion can apply to procrastination. Viewing your productivity (or lack thereof) as an equation is helpful because it allows you to think through the variables present in your life and learn how to manipulate them. First, an object at rest tends to stay at rest, while an object in motion tends to stay in motion (the first step is the hardest step). Next, the amount of work produced is a product of the focus and the force that is applied toward it (focus your efforts intentionally). Finally, for every action, there is an equal and opposite reaction (take inventory of the productive and unproductive forces present in your life).

- Another factor in procrastination is the paradox of choice, wherein choices and options are actually detrimental because they cause indecision and plague us with doubt. They might even cause us to act like Buridan's donkey and proverbially starve to death between two dishes of food. To combat this, get into the habit of setting a time limit on your decisions, making matters black and white, aiming to become satisfied, and immediately picking a default option.

- Finally, understand that motivation and the mood to stop procrastinating is not something that appears spontaneously. It may never appear... *before* the fact. But after you get started, it will almost always appear. Motivation *follows* action, yet most of us are seeking motivation that *creates* action. We are doing it backward and just need to get started to feel better, more often than not.

Chapter 4: Psychological Tactics

- Sometimes it's necessary to trick ourselves into doing what we don't want to. In fact, that's a primary aspect of improving and practicing anything. We are momentarily seduced by the benefit or end result to the point where we can grin and bear the present pain.

- Many of us think we can only work when we are in the mood for it or when inspiration strikes us. That is a losing battle. Don't rely on your mood to get you where you want to go. Instead, think the opposite way: once you begin action, your mood will follow. To get to action quicker, think in terms of low thresholds to get started, as well as focusing only on the process and not the end product. Also, forgive yourself for procrastinating, and instead of thinking about the problem, think about the possible checklist of solutions.

- Understand and tame omission bias. This is when you realize that it's easy to feel the impact of doing something but not the impact of skipping something. This is about more than awareness; you can battle omission bias with proactive visualization of the bad future you are creating. That will kick you into gear.

- Visualize your future self. Most of us suffer from *temporal myopia,* which is when you are nearsighted with regards to time. But your everyday actions can lead you to vastly different futures. Think about your future self; when you can effectively visualize the personal consequences of your actions (positive and negative) in excruciating detail, you are more aware of what you need to do and more impacted by it.

- Finally, use if-then statements. These make procrastination difficult because the decisions are made beforehand. If a certain daily event occurs, then you will start working in some aspect. When behaviors are chained together and tied to concrete milestones, they become easier.

Chapter 5: Strategic Planning

- Even though we know procrastination is always lurking, we can't always fight it, no matter how close attention we pay. That's why it pays to plan to avoid procrastination completely. At least you'll give yourself a much better fighting chance.
- First, you can use the STING method, by which you select one task, time yourself, ignore everything else, opt for no breaks, and give yourself a reward. It's the act of willful ignorance that makes STING so powerful. This is a scary concept, but once you resolve to only juggle one thing at a time, you'll be happy to report that the world didn't end. You'll find that you can create STING periods, and start chaining them together with breaks between. With luck, it will become your new normal.
- Second, you can use your knowledge of the procrastination equation to your advantage by increasing both success expectancy ("I can do it") and task value ("This is worthwhile") while decreasing reward delay ("I see no immediate

benefit") and impulsiveness (the *need* to engage in something). You can manipulate each of these variables to increase your motivation and momentum toward productivity. At the very least, you can recognize what factors you may be ignoring.

- Third, you can bundle temptations. This means simultaneously satisfying the hedonist in your current self and the prudence of your future self. Make both happy at the same time by pairing unpleasant tasks (future self) with sought-after pleasures (present self). You can create a win-win situation; you can also do this in the negative sense by doling out small punishments to yourself in the absence of action.

- Finally, you can use the Eisenhower matrix to distinguish between urgent and important tasks. They may overlap from time to time, but ultimately, if you are procrastinating, you are focusing too much on urgent to the detriment of important.

Chapter 6: Structuring Against Procrastination

- This chapter is about how to structure your day to prevent procrastination. Will it work every time, every day? No, but you stand a much better chance when you engage in these exercises than when you don't. Procrastination leaps on you when you have idle time and when you're unengaged. Scheduling and structuring prevents this and attempts to take the decision out of your hands entirely.
- The first step in scheduling is more about how to approach your schedule and day structure. Namely, pledge to yourself to have no more "zero days," where a zero day is a day that you've let slip by without doing anything to achieve your goal. You can also substitute an hour, week, or a minute in place of a day. In any case, having the intention to just act in every time segment will help prevent procrastination.

- Self-interrogation questions can also help you when you're on the cusp of procrastinating. If you ask yourself a certain set of questions, you are able to immediately take a step and break through the inertia. The questions are as follows: What is one thing I can do right now? What are my top three priorities today? How can I make this easier for me to follow through? And what will go wrong if I don't try to persevere?

- Truly scheduling everything into your agenda works because it lets you visually understand what needs to be done. This effect can be further enhanced if you schedule, along with the task itself, where you will perform it, what resources are needed, and when it should be done. The more details and specificity, the better. You can take this a step further by living in your calendar and accounting for all of your 168 hours a week.

- Finally, you can limit your information consumption. Very little of what we consume is helpful or even relevant. Most of it is also consumed unconsciously, without us realizing that we are spending so much time and effort on it—we get sucked in. Cultivate self-awareness and curate your consumption and reduce your media sources so you can devote your limited energy toward work and motion.

Chapter 7. Get Off Your Butt

- Getting off your butt might be the very essence of conquering procrastination. Procrastination's mortal enemy is the immediate, present moment. So how do we seize that?

- Utilize the 40–70 rule as popularized by Colin Powell. This rule states the following: you only need between 40% and 70% of the information, confidence, time, or preparation that you think you do. Anything else is just spinning your wheels and procrastinating, and 100% of what you want is impossible from the starting line. So take action at 70%, at worst, because things won't improve by simply waiting longer.

- Tiny steps are the best steps. Large tasks look intimidating and impossible. But when you break each boulder down into small pebbles that can be taken care of instantaneously and effortlessly, then you have a chance to build momentum and take care of what needs to be done in short order.

- We are full of excuses for the protection of our ego. But of course, excuses are detrimental to your working spirit. It's important to realize that these excuses are largely fabrications. "Not right now"—there is never a perfect time. "I'm not good enough"—no, but you can become good enough. "I don't know where to start"—start with what you can do right now, not only with an ultimate endpoint in mind.

- Pay attention to the energy pyramid. Energy, more than time and more than anything else, is what determines how much we get done. It is the scarcest resource because it drains on a daily basis. There are four aspects/levels to it, and each contributes to overall being able to focus and work: physical (no fatigue), emotional (no unhappiness), mental (no discouragement), and spiritual (no lack of purpose).

Once again, I would be highly, greatly, amazingly grateful and appreciative if you felt like taking just 30 seconds and leaving me a review on Amazon! Reviews are incredibly important to an author's livelihood, and they are shockingly hard to come by. Strange, right?

Anyway, the more reviews my books get, the more I am actually able to continue my first love of writing. If you felt any way about this book, please leave me a review and let me know that I'm on the right track. CLICK HERE TO REVIEW